The Notes of Adam's Song

W0038381

A Surviving Parent's Journey through the Valley of the Shadow of Death

A Roadmap from Grief and Bereavement, to

Recovery and Healing...for Surviving

Parents, and the People Who Care for Them

by

Joel Johnson, M.A.Ed.
Director

National Crisis Intervention Training Institute, Inc.

....A Surviving Parent...

8-20-20

To Christian —

Thank you for your desire to be a part of God's healing in the lives of hurting, surviving parents.

Love in a risen Lord & savior.

— Joel

Copyright 2020, Joel Johnson

"The Notes of Adam's Song: A Surviving Parent's Journey Through the Valley of the Shadow of Death"

---FIRST EDITION---

ISBN: 978-0-578-64036-5

is a *"Way Out of the Box" Publication of the National Crisis Intervention Training Institute, Inc.*

PO Box 54   Alva, OK 73717
Contact Phone: 405-543-9221

E-mail: JJohnson@NCITI.org
www.NCITI.org

Page	Table of Contents (NOTE: Poetry in *Italics*)

In Loving Memory of

Adam Joshua Johnson

On this earth July 31, 1984 – January 8, 2009

"Son, your smile is our melody; your heart is our harmony;
And the lyrics of your life, they make us strong.
Our love for you will stay, and will never go away,
For we are the Notes of Adam's Song."

Foreword

As an artist, the complex job of a poet is to paint details with words; to draw for readers an elaborate scene with a few mere strokes of his brush. His words become his paint, as pigments embody a thought or a person with many colors, or a simple hue. Taking this responsibility to heart, Joel Johnson has strived to become an adept artist. In *"The Notes of Adam's Song,"* my dear friend Joel, through his colorful depiction of comedy, drama, pathos, tragedy, inspiration, and prophetic muse, shares many of his most-precious life lessons: the importance of telling loved ones how much they have affected our lives; how healing can be painful, but how the pain makes our world more rich and vivid; the healing power of encouragement and mercy; how beautiful love truly is; and that, perhaps the most important parts of being *"Created in God's Image"* are the gifts of *"Creativity"* and *"Sense of Humor."*

For the past several years, through the auspices of the *National Crisis Intervention Training Institute*, I have been privileged to know Joel as friend, colleague, co-writer, co-trainer, and creative partner. I wholeheartedly invite you to explore his anthology: a veritable gallery of poetry, prose, and memoirs. Walk the halls and gaze your eyes, minds, and hearts upon pictures of some of the most important principles we both strive to live by, in an effort to contribute to what Joel refers to as a *"kinder, gentler, and more loving world."*

As a writer, educator, trainer, and human rights activist who loves language, and what artists like Joel can create with it, I have been asked by him on several occasions to review his writing with a critic's red pen in hand. I have thoroughly enjoyed the task. I hope you enjoy the following pages, and incorporate it within your own vision and life experience. I also hope that the included pieces enrich your life as much as they have mine. I remain,

Respectfully Yours,

Rebecca "Doc" Simcoe, Ph.D.

Dear Reader,

When your parents die, they call you an *"orphan;"* when your spouse dies, they call you a *"widow"* or a *"widower;"* but, when your child dies, there's no word for that. Why? Because it is so obscenely unnatural to outlive your child, that the experience defies description. Prior to January 8, 2009, I thought I understood what it meant to lose something precious; however, I didn't have a clue. I had suffered losses before, and as the parent of a mentally-ill child, had experienced many fleeting, fearful moments, worrying that I might one day get the call telling me that *"the other shoe had dropped."* I had thought about what my world would be like, if one day it was tragically cut short, but I never had an inkling as to how truly horrible the pain might be.

Even as a police detective working crimes against children, I didn't fully understand the pain of losing a child. Over the years, I had worked with hundreds of parents who had suffered the *"worst of the worst"* tragedies in life. I strived to be supportive as possible, as I helped them cope with the depth, intensity, and everlasting impact of their pain. Not until the death of my son, however, did I know what they were going through.

It is my hope that, out of my experience, my fellow Surviving Parents may find help, hope, and healing, and that other readers may become better equipped to support parents who have suffered the most horrible of nightmares. I pray that this book will help to fulfill a vision my Son had: to challenge others to bring hope and help to a lost and dying world. This was his life's goal, and is now my legacy to pass on to you.

As you read this book, it will become obvious to you that, rather than progressing in chronological order, my story moves back and forth in time, much like the grief process does. Also, from time to time, certain autobiographical accounts (e.g. how Adam died) are deliberately repeated, to provide foreshadowing or explanatory background, and/or to explain the complex events and co-morbidity factors that eventually led to Adam's death. At other times, breaches in chronology or repetition will occur, in order to allow some comic relief to you, the reader --when I believe it is needed the most—and/or to expose my state of mind at the time the account was originally added into the manuscript.

Finally, in certain areas, this book comments on my personal spiritual and religious views. However, as you read, I hope it will become obvious that I am not trying to cram my own beliefs down the throats of readers who believe differently, who participate in other religions, or who are agnostics or atheists.

I openly address why and how people become angry at, or come to question their concept of God…wondering why and/or how a Loving God could allow death to happen to their child. I only ask you to read this book with an open mind and heart. It is designed to bring you peace and healing, regardless of your own personal beliefs. I hope you are helped and blessed, as we journey together, and that, if you are in need of healing, you find it within these pages. Thank you for taking the time to glimpse into the extraordinary life of my Son, and for joining me as we *"listen to his Song"* together. *...Adam's Dad*

Grateful Acknowledgements

Just as my grief and bereavement are works in progress, so has been the writing of this book. My life, from now until I get to play another duet with Adam, has been blessed by so many people. I cannot list them all, but wish to offer thanks to family members and friends who have been especially helpful to me in my adventurous, yet excruciating journey:

- First and foremost, **my Blushing Bride, Barb.** Thank you for your patience, compassion, understanding, support, and steadfast love. I don't deserve you. Adam loved you so very, very much, honey.

- **Debra Alford**, my first wife, Adam's Mom, my dear friend, and my partner in grief. I love you, Deb. Only you truly know what I'm feeling. Thanks for being the *"World's Best Mom."*

- **Andrea Brakebill,** Adam's birth mother, **Kamberly and Paden Smith** and **David Brakebill,** Adam's birth-siblings. Andrea, words cannot express how much we are grateful to you for the gift of life you gave to our Son, and your selfless sacrifice. **Gary Brakebill (in Heaven)**, for being such an incredible Dad to Kamberly and David.

- **"Mom and Dad" Delores and Bill Anthony (in Heaven)**, my foster parents, as well as my sisters, **Pam LeGrand** and **Sandy Chichester**, and your beautiful families. You took me in as your own when I was 17 years old. Thank you for always being there for me. I love you so much.

- **My brother Ken Johnson, my former sister-in-law Jeri**

13

Ross, and my niece and nephew, Mallory Moreno and Jordan Johnson. Thank you for your love and support, especially during the first days of our loss. Ken, we went through so much together when we were growing up. Because of you, I was never alone, and I'm not now.

- **Linda, Steve, Di Di, Ed, Dan, Glenn, Joan, Natalie, Gregg, Ian, Paul, Elizabeth**, and all the other members of Deb's family who been such a strong support system for her, and for Adam throughout his entire life. Thank you for your prayers in my direction, as well.

- **Janita M. Ardis, MD** and **John McBee, PhD** for taking care of Adam. I know you did your best to help him.

- My dear friend, therapist-when-I-need-one, and esteemed colleague, **Jim Bogan, LCSW, and his beautiful wife, Judy**. I love you both more than you know. Thank you for loving Adam since he was a pup, and for taking such good care of him when he was your client. Oh, and Jim? *Who says I never take you anyplace nice?*

- To **Kathy Morgan, Judy Giovannetti, Carol Parsley (in Heaven), Beth Talbot, Beth Rosenthal,** and the rest of my CRA Family. Thank you for loving Adam.

- **Teresa Arruza**, my beloved former partner in *The Moon Glow Duo*. Thanks to you, each time I hear our CD's, I experience healing.

- **Pastor Israel Hogue, formerly of *"The Edge"* Church** (Adam's friend and Pastor), and **Adam's Church Family at *The Edge Church***. Israel, your words of comfort, and your love and appreciation for Adam will never be forgotten. Thanks for hearing Adam's *"Battle Cry,"* and for giving him the opportunity for ministry.

- **Cindy Webster,** a dear friend who gave me comfort and support just after Adam's death, and throughout the course of our friendship. Cindy, thanks for referring me to *"The Shack."* You are always in my heart. I love you.

- **My "Little Brother" Chris Crabtree**, who dragged me *"out of my shell"* in the weeks after Adam's death…and to **Teddy D. Wright, Esme Russell, Franki Markstone,** and all the other beautiful people in that special place in St. Pete. You embraced me in your loving hearts during that dark time. I love you, and will never forget you.

- **Dawn Skonecki**, my wonderful little friend, who is cute as a button, and has been so supportive. Through your gifts of love and kindness, you truly taught me that *"someone small can greatly care."* Did I mention that you're funny? Well, if not, YOU'VE mentioned it many times. Uh…okay, I get it. You're funny.

- **Ciara Martin,** my unofficially-adopted granddaughter. You are one of the most beautiful souls I have ever known. Your strength, determination, and life are an inspiration. I could not be prouder. Papa Joel loves you!

- **Greg Giltner, Chief of Police, Oklahoma Christian University Police Department / former Chaplain and Sergeant, Oklahoma City Police Department,** who has remained an ongoing source of support and encouragement since the early months after Adam's death, and who has, over the years, become a dear friend.

15

Greg, thank you for your continued assistance to Chris.

- **Bill Citty (Chief of Police, Ret.), Captain "Bo" Matthews, (Homicide Commander), Johnny Kuhlman, (Assistant Chief of Police), and Captain Bill Weaver (Training Commander), of the Oklahoma City Police Department**, for your assistance and sensitivity when meeting with us (along with **Sgt. Giltner**) to offer your condolences, and to listen to us, and answer our questions, following Adam's death.

- The **Masih Family: Alishbah, Ruby, Miriam**, and **Gulshan (in Heaven),** for your love and daily prayers. It is humbling that, in spite of your tremendous suffering and adversity, you pray for us. We love you all very much. Ruby and Miriam, your *"Joel Dad"* and *"Mom Barb"* are so proud and blessed to be considered your parents. Gulshan, I know you are now with Adam.

- **My adopted Amish family** in Alaska, **Buddy and Rachel Matson**, and…here goes: **Edward, Aaron, Elise, Adam, Hannah, Abigail, Isaac, and Nathanael**. Thank you for your faithful daily prayers, for as long as I have known you. I love you. Thanks for making me an *Honorary Amish Guy! ..."MacGyver."*

- **Students, faculty, staff, and colleagues** at **Mid-America Christian University** and **Northwestern Oklahoma State University**, for your faithful support over the last six years. It's been an honor to serve and protect. And, a special thanks to **Frankie Heath**, for those beautiful words you spoke to me in 2016: *"And now you have us."*

16

- My professional *"Partner in Crime,"* **Deputy Diana L. Jones, Cleveland County (OK) Sheriff's Office (Ret.),** and her beloved life partner, **Belinda Foster,** for your faithful friendship, support, and invaluable assistance in building NCITI.

- **Members of the Advisory and Governing Boards** of NCITI, Inc. Thank you for your contributions to the organization's success. We could not do it without you!

- **Rebecca "Doc" Simcoe, PhD,** for your wisdom, expertise, sensitivity, friendship, and the beautiful *"Foreword"* you wrote for this book. I love you.

- **D.P. "Pat" Hutton (in Heaven),** my dear friend, collaborator, and my *"Soke."* I miss you dearly. Thank you for your friendship, love, and devotion, Brother.

- **Dee Chambers,** for your undying friendship, support, and sense of humor, when I've really needed it. Like Adam, in spite of your own pain, diversities, and challenges, you have never forgotten to care for me.

- **To B.J. Tumlinson,** who inspired me to be a writer, and who provided me with so much encouragement and support during my early, difficult H.S. years. Thank you so much for all you gave to me and taught me.

- **Liberty Devitto,** who inspired Adam. You were his hero, Liberty. He never forgot getting to jam with you.

- **Kerri Griffin-Mims and her husband John, Judy and Jim Giovannetti, David and Christina Villarreal, Tera Idleman, Jim and Alicia Maisano, Kelvin and Debra**

Winter, Shawn Prosser South, William "Ponch" Alves, and my countless other fellow **Surviving Parents.** I hurt for you, with you, and I love you.

- Our pets, **Punchbowl, Simba, Monkey,** and the rest of our menagerie, who have crossed *"The Rainbow Bridge,"* for keeping me on my toes. **Shady**, Adam loved you best. I know you're sitting at his feet right now, with that dim-light bulb look on your face, not quite having figured out where you are, but being comforted by Adam's presence.

- *Last but certainly not least, special gratitude to **God's Invisible Emissaries from Heaven**, who faithfully watched over and protected Adam, while he was here on earth; And most of all, to our **Lord Jesus Christ and Father God**, who Graciously Received Adam on that tragic, dark, and cold morning of January 8, 2009.*

And to a young man who has remained in our prayers for the past eleven years:
A SPECIAL ACKNOWLEDGEMENT:

To Chris Hortness, former Sergeant, Oklahoma City Police Department. You have our forgiveness, understanding, and prayers. We know you have been impacted terribly by Adam's death. I pray that, reading this book, you'll be blessed by his life. **We are here for you, Chris. Any time you're ready.**

….A Special Message for Those of You Who Give Me Hope…
.

You Are My Precious 'Home of Hearts'

When I am caught in cold, dark storms;

When tears build up, and sadness forms,

I enter in to *"Special Rooms"*
Where light abounds; no darkness looms.

I go into a Special Place
Where I am warmed by God's Sweet Grace;
Where love and peace are found in spite
Of cold and dark, foreboding night.

I feel at home, because I know
That love lies there like fallen snow.
In there, I always find God's Peace.
In there, I see the darkness cease.

Fear disappears without a trace;
A log glows in the warm fireplace.
The sadness melts; no fear can hide
Inside those rooms where I reside.

It's through those rooms I find relief;
They comfort me through forlorn grief.
They build me up and offer hope
When ends my grasp on my life's rope.

Sometimes, God gives to me a Sign;
Sometimes He puts Peace in my mind;
Sometimes, through Scripture, comfort grows;
Sometimes, through those rooms, God's Love flows.

For those of you who often view
My poetry, this shan't seem new:
You're used to my symbolic rhyme,
So here is one more teaching time:

You know I'm one for metaphors;
I use them to pry open doors.
So, here's the truth, the *"Rooms"* are YOU,
Dear friends that God brings Comfort through.

So, it should come as no surprise
That through this rhyme a lesson lies.
I can't resist; I can't control
How poetry helps heal my soul.

God speaks to me through *you* dear folks;
Sometimes through prayers; sometimes through jokes;
Sometimes through comfort found in words;
Sometimes in tales of soaring birds.

And then, in turn, I lie and write,
Oft in the middle of the night.
Upon my phone, I plant my thumb;
My thoughts are wise; my typing dumb.

Espec'lly, when I'm really tired,
Yet, through your postings I'm inspired

By your sweet gestures, reaching out,
To ease my pain as I cry out.

I never cease to be amazed
That you are there, when I'm half-crazed.
You always grant a Place to rest:
A Haven when I face the test

Of all I know that's safe and true.
No matter what I'm going through,
You always seem to come around,
And in your warmth God's Peace is found.

My friends, you play a special role
In comforting my painful soul.
Through you, God grants a place to rest;
To gather strength; to be God's Best.

You fill my heart with hope and love;
You bring me Peace from God Above.
My world's a kinder, gentler place,
Because, through you, I sense God's Grace.

I'm privileged to call you *"Home."*
You're there, no matter where I roam.
Where comfort lies, where gladness starts,
You Are My Precious "Home of Hearts."
Copyright 2015, Joel Johnson

Chapter One

From Dad to Son, On January 11, 2020

Dear Adam,

Son, I began writing this book ten years ago today --on my birthday-- one year after you left this earth. I have finally finished the manuscript, which is now ready to be proofread, edited, and published. It took ten years, because, as has been my journey of recovery, this book's birth has been a very long, painful, revealing, and healing process. Some of the chapters of the book couldn't have been written any sooner than they were. Now, it's time to share my memories with a lost and dying world, with fellow Surviving Parents, and the people who love them.

I dedicate this book to you, Adam. From now to beyond Eternity, I will love you, remember you, and carry you in my heart. To this day, I often carry on the two-way dialog with which we always ended our talks. Come on, Son…join me. You know the words: *"Love you, Son." "Luv ya, too." "I love you, My Son." "I love you, My Dad." "And I like the way you talk." "I like the way you talk, too…eh, hehhhh."* Of course, it has, on more than one occasion, taken some explaining to keep other people from calling the guys in the white coats to come get your Dad, when they hear me reciting both parts, in different voices. ***I love you, Buddy Boy.***

By the way, a while back, I found your *"Battle Cry for a New Christian Initiative"* buried on my laptop, as well as one of your almost-finished Songs: *"Home."* Their discovery was such a gift from God, when I needed it the most. In this book, I'm sharing your *"Battle Cry"* with the world --or at least with those who look at my websites, attend my seminars, and/or who read this book. I've read your manifesto many times since your death, and I never cease to be blessed by it. I've heard from others who have read it, and have been blessed, as well. You ARE making a difference, Son, and will continue to, as long as new *"Notes"* are added to your *"Song"* each day. I am so very proud of you.

On the next page are the lyrics to the Song I wrote for you, the night before your funeral. For obvious reasons, I was crying too hard to sing it during the service, and, in fact, was barely able to even recite its lyrics during your Eulogy. Your Mom put the refrain of the Song on the tombstone where your shell is buried, near the train tracks, in the cemetery beside your old alma mater: Edmond North H.S. It's peaceful there, Son. You'd like it, if you were there. When I go there, it always reminds us of how you loved to watch the choo-choo trains go by, when you were a little guy. I love you, Buddy. Always have; always will.

Love,

Your Dad

P.S.   Anyway, here are the lyrics to your Song:

The Notes of Adam's Song

You came to us one day, in your very special way;
Sent from God, you helped us to belong.
You taught us how to give, and you made us want to live
Better lives through the beauty of your Song.

Your smile is the melody; your heart is the harmony;
And the lyrics of your life: they make us strong.
Our love for you will stay, and will never go away,
For we are the Notes of Adam's Song.

You tuned in to our pain, and your love for us remained;
You taught us how to laugh and how to cry.
Though you hurt, you made us smile, with your special
"Adam style,"
And your mischief, and the twinkle in your eye.

Your smile is the melody; your heart is the harmony;
And the lyrics of your life: they make us strong.
Our love for you will stay, and will never go away,
For we are the Notes of Adam's Song.

Your passion for your beliefs will comfort us in grief;
Loved by God, you rest safely in His Arms.
Now, never will you cry; the tears have left your eyes:
No more fear; no more pain; free from harm.

Yes, Son, your smile is our melody; and your heart is our harmony;

And the lyrics of your life, they make us strong.

Our love for you will stay, and will never go away,

For We Are the Notes of Adam's Song.

Copyright 2009, Joel Johnson

A "Surviving Parent's" Job Description

An hour before the sun rose on the morning of January 8, 2009, my world --as I knew it-- ended, when I received a phone call from Debbie, my Son's mother. It's been eleven years since that day, but I still sometimes wake up in a cold sweat, hearing Debbie's trembling, frightened, tearful voice, saying, *"Oh, Joel, Adam's been shot."* I remember the horrible combination of shock, denial, panic, fear, anxiety, and deep nausea that wreaked havoc over every fiber of my being, as I curled into a ball and wept. Two and a half hours later, the phone call came from someone at the Oklahoma City Police Department, confirming that Adam was indeed dead.

Credit: Daily Oklahoman January 8, 2009

At that moment, I lost all joy, hope, and peace; my sense of purpose and meaning, and my sense of humor, left me. At that moment, I lost the most important portion of my identity, because, of all the responsibilities, roles, and relationships in my life, NONE compared to the all-important role of being *"Adam's Dad."* Since that day, it has been a very difficult and always-painful transition to move from *"Ex-Dad"* to *"Veteran Dad,"*

27

and, eventually, to *"Surrogate Dad,"* to a handful of young people who asked me to fill their father's absence in their lives.

For over a decade, I have learned much, and, most importantly, have had the privilege of being used as an instrument of God's Peace in the lives of other *"Surviving Parents."* I am currently travelling a painful journey, still on a road that no parent should ever have to walk upon. While I have made some considerable progress in the last several years, I still sometimes stumble on that rocky road toward soulful redemption. I have lived through devastation, ultimate heartbreak, and the utter destruction of my soul. As of today, I still have my bad days and some good ones, but have yet to experience the joy that I felt when my Son was with me here on earth.

As a recipient of God's Mercy, I am gradually learning to integrate that most-terrible experience into my life; in order to allow God to fulfill my Son's legacy through me. I will never *"get over"* this tragedy, but, by His Hand, I'm confident I will continue to work through it, day by day.

An all-important part of my healing has been experienced in my music and my writing…especially my poetry. I now understand, respect, and appreciate the importance of learning to create a *"living tribute"* for departed loved ones: our parents, spouses, friends, grandparents, and especially, our children. One of the goals of this book is to serve as a model for other Surviving Parents' living memorials, honoring their deceased children. Equally as important, I have come to realize that life, while precious, is oft-times cut short, and is unpredictable. I have come to truly appreciate the importance of telling and showing loved ones what they mean to me…and why that is important.

I hope you enjoy this flowing stream of my own personal creativity, and that you will find at least a few golden nuggets buried in its proverbial sand. I thank each and every one of you for your interest, kindness, support, and your contribution to my healing, as well as the healing of other Surviving Parents. I have been inspired by many of you to write *"tribute poems,"* which are contained in another poetry anthology, entitled *"Tributes."*

Six years after Adam's death, at Tinker Air Force Base, I was speaking to a military veteran of the Korean War, who is a Purple Heart recipient, and a Disabled American Veteran. After I thanked him for his meritorious service and his sacrifice, he asked me if I had ever served in the military. I shared with him that, when I was a youth, my eyesight had prohibited me from entering military service, but that I had later served as a police officer and paramedic. We talked a little bit more, and the topic turned to family. He then asked if I had any children.

Things then got a bit more personal, as I told him about the death of my Son, Adam. At that time, I told him I was still involved in law enforcement, as an instructor and technical consultant; however, at that time, I was not actively serving on a police department. Since that time, however, I have been *"dragged, kicking and screaming…back into active-duty law enforcement."* On that particular day, I told the military veteran that the role I miss far more than being a police officer or paramedic, was the profound privilege of serving as a *"Dad."*

He asked, *"Young man, did you perform your duties honorably, as a police officer, paramedic, and as a father?"* I told him that I did my best to do so. The old soldier then said seven words to me, five of which I utter to both active duty and veteran members of the military on an almost-daily basis. He said, *"Well, Son, thank you for YOUR service."* I'll never forget the powerful feelings that I experienced when I heard those words spoken by that wise, old Hero. I'm not sharing this to toot my own horn, or to drop a hint for accolades or compliments. I share that account as an introduction to a discussion of the purposes of pain, suffering, loss, and feelings of absolute insignificance.

Pain, contrary to popular belief, is not our enemy. This truth applies to our experiences with trauma, addiction, loss, and the temptation to take one's own life…when psychological, emotional, spiritual, or physical pain gets to be unbearable. Pain is our friend. While numbness is often sought after --or simply occurs-- it sometimes seems to be a welcome response to stimuli which causes pain, such as illness, injury, or traumatic events in our lives, or, especially, death of a child. We must remember, though, that numbness is not merely the absence of pain; it is the total loss of feeling. It's also important to remember that pain is not always caused by trauma; it is sometimes a symptom of healing; it still hurts, but it is worth it.

Let me confess something: God speaks to me a lot…sometimes in some pretty weird and comical places. He's taught me several important life lessons in the bathroom, for example. Like any other self-respecting adult male who views time in the bathroom as a retreat to a welcome oasis of solitude, peace, and quiet --as well as a stolen opportunity to read non-mandatory reading material-- I have been guilty, upon occasion, of spending too much time reading in the *"library,"* or getting carried away browsing on my smart phone. As a result, I've occasionally had the unpleasant experience of sitting there too long, then suddenly realizing that one of my legs had turned totally numb.

When that occurs, my routine is always the same: I attempt to stand up, finding that it is difficult to do so when one of my feet does not feel the floor. When I finally muster up enough courage to bear weight with my numb leg, I usually find that at least one of my legs either goes totally out from under me, or begins to engage in clumsy, uncontrollable Elvis-like gyrations. My usual tendency is to then grab ahold of the bathroom cabinet, and to stand there with the deadened foot slightly lifted off the floor, as I wait in dread for what I know is coming next: those thousands of *"pins and needles"* which light my leg up like a Christmas tree, as blood circulation and nervous innervation are restored. It is a maddeningly-excruciating experience, but it is a sign that my leg is *"coming back to life."*

Moral of the story: Numbness, even if it brings about a total lack of pain, is not the same as life and good health. In fact, it can be a terrible sign that a part of you is dying. Pain, on the other hand, is not always because of trauma, but is sometimes a symptom of healing. In a very real sense, pain is our friend, because it tells us four truths that, if we forget one or more of them, our lives may be threatened. It tells us something is wrong; something needs to change; if change does not occur, our lives, or overall health, may be at risk; and, it tells us we are still alive.

A key element to healing, and to regaining a sense of

purpose and meaningful identity, is to somehow become *"significant"* again, to integrate our losses into our lives, and to find a compelling reason to live. In my life's journey since Adam's death, I have experienced this on several levels: making the transition from being an *"Ex-Parent"* to becoming a *"Veteran Parent."* While the pain caused by my Son's death is sometimes still indescribably excruciating, it is a vital part of my own personal healing.

Emotional, psychological, and spiritual healing is sometimes painful, but I am coming to understand that the results make it well worth it. Just like nerves coming back to life, as numbness leaves, the restoration of feeling is sometimes very painful. It is, nevertheless, a clear sign of restoration-in-progress. Healing pain is a different kind of pain; it is a type that holds hope of recovery...while the pain that stems from the void left by such a catastrophic loss of a child is so terrible that, if numbness is achieved, Surviving Parents are sometimes afraid to feel again. They often seek out numbness, avoiding emotional bonding at all costs, due to fear of repeated loss. That type of pain is one which is magnified by a coupling feeling of despair.

The despair-based pain can come from a variety of co-morbidity factors that bring us to believe that we are no longer whole human beings. In some cases, a key co-morbidity factor in suicide is a sense of loss of identity and purpose. For example: If one's sole sense of purpose lies in being a parent, and that person loses his or her only child, the Surviving Parent can come to feel that the hole that was once filled by that loving relationship will never again be filled by anything --or anyone-- else.

In that state of suffering, Surviving Parents often feel that they are no longer whole: that they are discarded, insignificant, and empty. It is common for those individuals to resort to methods of numbing themselves, to insulate them from the terrible pain stemming from their traumatic loss; at least, for a while. That can make any other form of intimate relationship very difficult to sustain, and is one of the key reasons that upwards to 80% of Surviving Parents' marriages oft-times end in divorce or estrangement, following the death of a child --usually within a five-year period following the child's death.

An explanatory comparison lies in the tragic phenomenon which sometimes occurs when healers, helpers, and heroes lose their ability to work in their chosen profession; especially if their entire sense of identity and self-worth once revolved around their professional identity being equated with their personal identity. Once they lose the ability to continue in their life's work, they sometimes come to feel that they no longer have a reason to exist. This is particularly true of our nation's heroes: military, law enforcement, EMS, and firefighting personnel, for example.

Losing the ability to work, they become severed from the comradery, sense of purpose, and sense of accomplishment which came from doing their duty. They often feel discarded, expendable, and worthless. As much as they are reminded by well-intended supporters that they are still remembered, they, at best, feel like useless *"has-beens."* And, in fact, they may be seen that way by myopic people in their own former profession.

They are, however, Treasures, nonetheless. I believe there is a way for discarded treasures to once again play a valuable role in society, and to discover that they are much more than the sum total of their curriculum vitae, or even the sum total of their mistakes, failures, or their professional accomplishments. While they may never be able to function in their old professional capacity, they can still make a positive difference in the world around them, thus becoming *"restored to significance."*

I also believe that at least partial healing and restoration is possible for parents who survive their children, even though there is nothing more obscenely-unnatural than for parents to outlive their children. My hope and prayer for my fellow Surviving Parents, is that they can somehow make the transition from being an *"Ex-Parent"* to being a *"Veteran Parent,"* and can learn to integrate the tragedy of their loss into their once-again-meaningful lives, as I have begun to do.

Late in life, helping them to do so has become an important part of *"my calling."* And so, I say to you, my friends who have honorably served as parents, but who now, due to tragic loss, are wounded veterans: *"Thank you for your service."* This book is especially written for YOU. Through it, may you find comfort, healing, guidance, and purpose; and may you be restored to significance. On June 15th of 2015, a few days after visiting with the Korean War combat veteran, I wrote the following poem.

Before talking to that old Hero, I just didn't have it in me to write this poem, or to even use the word *"blessed"* in a sentence describing me. Now I know I am blessed. I had the joy and privilege of having served *"active duty"* as a *"Dad"* for over 24 glorious years. Many people don't get to experience that for even a few moments. Yes, what I had was a precious gift.

On Father's Day I Know I'm Blessed

It's always difficult, I've found,
Each year when this day comes around.
My heart cries out in deep dismay:
"On, No! Another Father's Day!"

Because I no more have the joy
Of being *"Dad"* to my dear boy;
Of each year sitting by the phone,
Knowing he'll call me on his own.

For twenty-four most-precious years,
I sat and wiped away the tears
Of joy, as I heard his sweet voice
Say he's so glad I made the choice

To be his Dad, and that his heart
Would love me 'til death would us part.
These last few years since his last breath,
I've countless times thought of his death,

With heartache, grief, and endless pain;
Wishing that we could talk again.
Though I was once fulfilled by him,
The loss has caused my light to dim.

I've seen myself no longer whole;
There's been within my very soul

A hole where light did once abide;
Where *"Dad"* and *"Son"* lived side-by-side.

Each year, I've faced with deepest dread
The task of telling folks he's dead,
When they inquire, *"Are you a Dad?"*
I do not want to make them sad;

And, yet, I've felt I would betray
My Son if I just brushed away
The question with a *"No"* or *"Yes."*
It's haunted me with deep distress.

But, then one day, I heard his voice
Say, *"Well done, Dad, you made the choice*
To proudly serve those many years."
I felt him wipe away my tears.

It still hurts deeply, and I cry
As thoughts do come of days gone by.
But now, at least, my heart reflects;
No longer am I just an *"Ex."*

So, on this day, I do now stand
With pride, as a *"Dad Veteran."*
He's placed a medal on my chest.
On Father's Day I Know I'm Blessed.

Dad and his Little Buddy at Disney World, 1989

Chapter Two

Adam's Hands

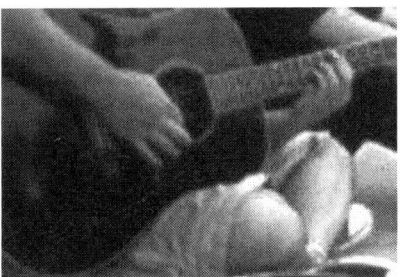

Adam, Busking in OKC Bricktown

At first glance, you probably never would have said that my father and I looked alike. I got most of my genetics from my mother's side of the family. For example, I think that the most my father ever weighed was *"right around"* 120 pounds. Suffice it to say, I weigh...uhh... more than that. When he was well into his eighties, my father still had more hair on his head than I did at age eighteen...long before I shaved my head. Our facial features and body types weren't similar, and yet...I have my father's hands: articulate fingers, widened at the middle joint, tapered with rounded finger-tip pads; *"musician's hands,"* my mother used to call them.

When he was way up there in years, a few years before he died, Dad lived with Barb and me for a while. At that point, he was having difficulty with many basic grooming tasks, so I would help bathe him, conduct his daily grooming, and help him trim his toenails and fingernails. I noticed that, when they got a bit too long, his fingernails grew like mine do if I wait too long to trim them...especially the ones on my forefingers. However, from the knuckles to the fingertips is pretty much where the physical resemblance between my father and me begins and ends.

In contrast, it always amazed me how much Adam and I looked alike. When it came to facial features and expressions, vocal inflections, coloring, and mannerisms, he was a proverbial *"chip off the old block."* I can't begin to tell you how many times we were told that we looked alike. I was amazed at the similarities…because Adam was adopted. The only explanation I could think of was that, just like people start looking like their dogs over time, the same may be true with dads and their adopted Sons.

But, as much as our facial features were alike, Adam didn't have my hands. While his were also very articulate, they were different from mine. Yet, my thoughts and observations about his hands have always played a key role in --and been emblematic of-- our very special relationship. From the moment I held him as a newborn for the first time, to the day of his funeral and burial --when I held his hand for the last time-- my life was blessed by the sight and touch of Adam's Hands.

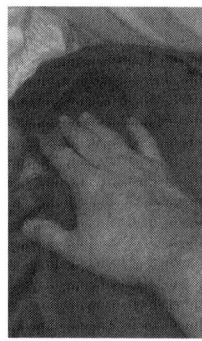

This is a picture of my hand resting on Adam's chest, when I first viewed his shell, after his death. You might find it inappropriate or even shocking that I would take pictures of Adam's body, let alone that I would put them in this book. I hope you can look past the social faux pas, and understand that this picture doesn't commemorate the last time I touched my Son; it merely documents the second to the last time I touched his shell. This picture was taken on my birthday, January 11, 2009, just after Barb and I arrived at the funeral home in Edmond, Oklahoma...to view Adam's shell for the first time after his death. Two days later, at his funeral, I once again placed my hand on his chest, kissed him goodbye, and then watched them close the lid to his casket.

At the funeral home, when I touched his chest, it was stiff and cold, yet I was reminded of when he was a baby: warm, alive, and full of wonder: a living miracle held in my own hands. My thoughts went immediately to a day when, as a Detective investigating crimes against children, I conducted a Sudden Infant Death Syndrome investigation. From *"The Day We Brought Him Home, Right Out of the Crate"* (Chapter Six), throughout his life, I would often get up in the middle of the night, and go into his bedroom to check on him while he was sleeping, and put my hand gently on his chest or back to make sure he was breathing okay. Then I would brush his little brow, cover him up, and go back to bed, thanking God for the blessing and privilege He had bestowed upon me by allowing me to be Adam's Dad.

Of course, this time, at the funeral home, he wasn't breathing, because he wasn't there; only his shell remained. If Adam had his way, there would have been a *"No One's at Home"* or *"Vacancy"* sign hanging around his neck. Or, as I mention

41

elsewhere in this book, he would have liked to have his shell seated upright, winking and grinning from ear to ear, while holding one hand up in a *"thumbs- up"* position, as he greeted people arriving for his funeral.

If there's one thing I've come to better understand and rely upon over the last several years, is that, while on earth, *we are not physical beings having a spiritual experience; we are spiritual beings having a physical experience.* Our physical bodies are merely erasable, pencil-drawn sketches of temporary housing...which, by the way, we are only renting, not buying. Our bodies belong to God. They are Temples of His Holy Spirit. Adam has long vacated the premises of his shell. Today and forever more, he is well beyond physical experiences here on earth. He's free. The tears caused by his pain and struggles here on earth have long ago been wiped from his eyes, forever. He's where there is, as the song goes: *"no more fear, no more pain, free from harm."*

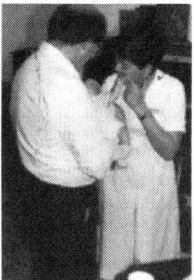 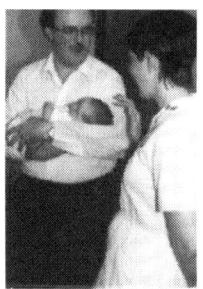

When he was a newborn, an infant, and then a toddler, I always marveled at how small, yet perfect his little hands were. Every detail was a miraculous piece of living art to me. I remember placing his tiny little hand on the palm of my own for the first time, when he was only two and a half days old, marveling

42

at both the contrast in size, and the perfection of God's Creation, as I succumbed to the temptation to further investigate, making sure he had just the right number of fingers, thumbs, and toes.

I remember how, just a few years later, as he began to take pride in becoming a *"big boy,"* he and I would gauge his growth --not so much by a height chart on the wall, or markings on the closet door frame-- but by how many of my fingers he could encompass with his little hand. When he was three years old, for example, he could wrap his hand around two of my fingers.

One of my favorite memories is described in Chapter Seven, when Adam settled down beside me on the bed one night at three o'clock in the morning, took two of my fingers into his own little hand, and held on for dear life as he drifted off to sleep after telling me, *"Dad, I can't sleep."* When I asked him why, he said, *"I need to talk."* Answering my response of *"Well, Son, what do you need to talk about at three in the morning?"* Adam responded, *"Dad, I've just got so many things going on."*

To this very day, as I recall looking at his peaceful, sleeping little face, the tears always come when I recall gazing down and looking at his hand holding mine. Reflecting on another special time, four years later, I recall when *"The Man with the T-Shirt"* story happened (Chapter 8). My memories always drift to how I held my crying little boy in my arms, was shattered to the core by the sight of his trembling little lower lip, as I told him about a Loving God who would surely honor a small child's pure-hearted prayer for a man who wore a blasphemous t-shirt (written about in Chapter Eight).

As a teenager, as Adam grew in stature, talent, and skill,

his hands were so strong, yet articulate…and oh, so talented when he picked up either a guitar, a set of drumsticks, or even a computer game control. When he would come up to me while I was hurting, placing his hand on my shoulder in a loving and supportive way, his hands were so comforting and healing. I always knew why: because he was silently praying for me.

As I've previously explained: even as a little boy, Adam never prayed out loud, but, believe me… he definitely prayed! I know he talks to our Heavenly Father about me today. Sometimes, I can almost feel his hand on my shoulder again. I know that he's talking to Jesus about me, because, even though I don't feel the physical touch of his hand, I feel the love, comfort, and support that always came with it. He would never say a word when he did it, yet I knew that he was talking to God about me.

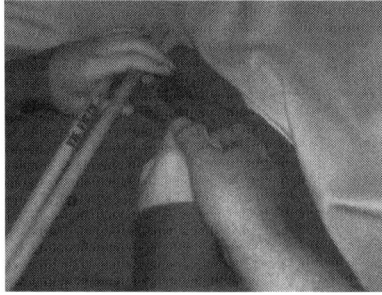

One very strange and sad thing: when he was still living in his shell, his hands were larger. Once Adam was no longer there; once his shell had been embalmed, his hands had shrunken. They were placed in a folded position on top of his stomach; holding his drumsticks. Yes, his hands were smaller, but not as small as they were the first time I held him in my arms, looked into his eyes, and thanked God for the greatest gift He had ever given me, aside from His Gift of Salvation.

Throughout childhood, adolescence, and adulthood, when I would go to pick him up to take him home with me, or any time we were riding together in a car after being separated for a while, Adam and I had a private ritual of holding hands, in silent celebration of our special relationship...of our bond as Dad and Son. We'd hold tight for a few minutes, fingers intertwined with each other's, then would squeeze each other's hand tightly, and finally let go. I would then say, *"I love you, my Son."* He'd say, as always, *"I love you, my Dad!"* That exchange was always followed by our reenactment of the aforementioned memorable verbal exchange between Karl Childers and little Frank Wheatley, in the movie *Sling Blade*: *"I like the way you talk,"* I'd say. Adam would then respond, *"I like the way you talk, too."* I don't think that anyone else ever truly *"got it"* when they overheard us. That's okay. *We* did.

Sometimes at night, when I'm lying in the dark, overwhelmed with the horrible sense of loneliness, loss, and emptiness that sometimes engulfs me like a cold, blackened wave, I try to think of Adam's hands. Out loud, I carry on both parts of our ritual Dad/Son conversation with each other, trying to mimic his voice as I'm reciting his part. I actually hold hands with myself, wrapping my fingers around each other, like the *"Here's*

45

the Church" hand position of the Church / Steeple poem. I close my eyes and squeeze tightly, trying to feel him, one more time.

I always cry when I do that, because it just never quite works; but I keep on trying, anyway. Then, I think of his hands once more; but this time, rather than imagining them being held in mine, I think of what I know in my heart-of-hearts to be true: that Adam's hand is *now* being held by Someone who loves him more than I ever could: A Risen Savior whose Hands are also quite remarkable, bearing scars caused by nails, driven into them over 2000 years ago. I realize at that point that Adam is in the *best* of Hands, and that nothing can ever remove him from their Eternal grasp.

Then, I usually think of the last time I physically touched Adam --when he was still alive in his shell-- on that perfect day in Arkansas, on Sunday, August 17, 2008…the last day I was physically with him here on earth. At about 2:30 in the afternoon, parked outside my travel trailer, I hugged him for the last time, looked into his smiling eyes, and then watched him get into his Jeep, and head out for Wyoming, waving at me out the window… as he drove away to yet another marvelous adventure.

It's ironic: the last part of his body that I ever saw was his left hand, waving farewell to his Dad, whom he loved and adored. I've memorized so many details of that wonderful day. In fact, that day was perfect, except for just one thing: it didn't last forever. Someday, though, I'll hold Adam's hand again, and will never let go. *That* day WILL last forever. I love Adam's hands. As long as I'm alive inside MY shell, I'll never forget them. They were --and are-- precious, comforting gifts from God.

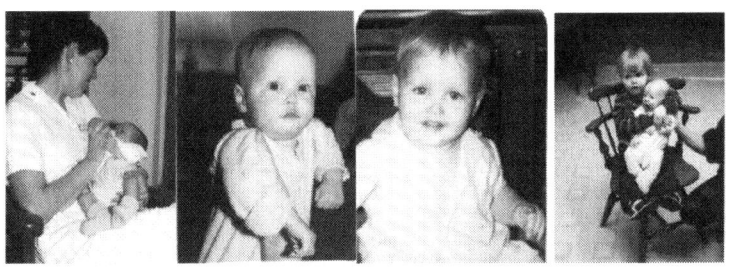

You Are Brand New, My Baby Boy

When you were brand new, Baby Boy,
I held your hand with so much joy.
I still recall my sense of awe
When for the first time, my eyes saw

How perfect was your little hand:
A feeling parents understand.
So tiny was it in my palm;
My spirit did it soothe, like balm.

It was my habit to come in
To your room, as you slept within;
To tuck you safely in your bed;
To look at you; oft tears were shed,

As I would place my hand upon
Your chest, to feel you breathe and warm.
Then, I would take your hand in mine
And gaze at you; my soul would shine.

When you were just a little tike,
Before you could command a bike,
We made a pact, as your grasp bound
My fingers, as you wrapped around

My own, first one, then two, then all.
One day your hand was not so small.
Your eyes lit up with light and joy.
You said, *"Now I am a BIG boy!"*

Then, later on, your hand grew large;
And suddenly, you could take charge.
As we arm wrestled, I was proud;
We'd grunt and groan, and laugh out loud.

As you grew older, when I felt
Your hand in mine, my heart would melt.
We felt such closeness, you and I.
But now, you live up in the sky.

You're now with God, forever more;
You live with him, with much in store.
For now, you know His Purest Joy.
You Are Brand New, My Baby Boy.

Chapter Three

To Add Insult to Injury, Grieving Isn't Funny

In Proverbs 3:5 (ESV), King Solomon told us to

"Trust in the Lord with all your heart, and do not lean on your own understanding."

That instruction does not tell us to quit using the brains that God gave us, but rather, to seek His Wisdom, placing ultimate faith in Him, rather than solely in our own *"head knowledge."* Quite honestly, to do so has always been a struggle for me; but I'm getting a little better at it, as I get older. I used to believe that if I could only understand something, I could overcome it.

Now I know better...but I don't always practice what I preach. In the past I was prone to attempting to *"battle my own demons"* by intellectualizing, and seeking practical solutions, based upon my own understanding. In doing so, I had a tendency to place my faith in myself and/or other human beings, rather than in God. This led to a lifelong problem of perfectionism. which a counselor once described to me as, *"a slap in the face of God."*

For many years, I was miserable, because I believed in God, but on a practical basis, I was placing my faith in someone or something other than God: myself. While I am a bit better at practicing Proverbs 3:5 in my everyday life today, I still sometimes relapse. As an example, on the day before Adam's funeral, I made a trip to a bookstore with my brother –which is an old tradition of ours whenever we get together. As soon as we hit the front doors of *Barnes and Noble*, I immediately made a beeline for the *"Self-Help"* and *"Psychology"* sections, and started looking at the books dealing with depression, death, dying, bereavement, and grieving. As I skimmed through book after book, I was overcome by how depressing that stuff was! I said to my brother, Ken, *"Wow! If you weren't depressed before, a quick browse through THIS horse-hockey will REALLY depress you."* Now don't misunderstand me…there is a lot of good stuff out there for people who have lost loved ones, and some of the material I browsed through seemed to be pretty good. But, so much of it, I found, was pure, unadulterated garbage.

Aside from the fact that some of the material on the *"grief and bereavement"* shelf was a bunch of bunk, just about everything I picked up…no, let me restate that: *everything* I picked up…was summarily not funny! Adam would definitely have had an issue with that one, and would have encouraged me to make this book as funny as possible, under the circumstances.

Keeping in mind that the *"sense of humor"* is just about the first thing to go when you're grieving, I thought to myself, *"Well, the old adage about 'With comedy, timing is everything,' seems to make sense."* Let me give you an example: Long before Adam's death, he and I were talking about some of the rollickingly hilarious *"mental hot feet"* we've given people down through the years (See Chapter Thirteen).

Adam told me that for his final mental hot foot, at his funeral, he wanted to be sitting up in his casket, eyes wide open, smiling lecherously, with his right hand in a *"thumbs up"* position, posthumously greeting the friends, family, and curiosity seekers who came piling in to pay tribute to his memory. He wanted a sign on an easel beside him, saying something like,

50

"Lighten up, folks! I ain't here!" Needless to say, while funny at the time, it would not have been funny at the funeral, to anyone; with the possible exceptions of my brother, Adam's pallbearers, and me. I confess that when I shared Adam's wishes with his mother, on January 11, 2009, it went over like a bad case of gas in a space suit.

Shortly after Adam had died, someone told me I might benefit from *"seeing someone."* I did some research on grief counseling and found out that about 40% of the people who had received grief counseling got worse after counseling, not better. Now, in all fairness to Grief and Bereavement Counselors, I realized that, just because a person got worse after grief counseling, the counseling wasn't necessarily to blame for their client's grief worsening.

On the other hand, people who got better *might* have done so IN SPITE OF inept grief counseling, not because of it. Or, their clinical improvement may have had nothing to do with the counseling...good or bad. Recognizing this, I started looking in greater detail at what kinds of material counselors go over with Surviving Parents, and how they deliver their material; and guess what? They weren't funny, either.

Oh, speaking of being a researcher --and of bad timing-- when Adam died, I was in the middle of the final pre-dissertation stages of my Ph.D. program (before I dropped out for financial reasons). I was supposed to be taking my Comprehensive Examination the week Adam was killed. I backed out of the process when Adam died, and three months later re-enrolled to take my Comprehensive Exam. Anyway, there are three questions that I had to answer in a 28-day period of time. I had to write a total of 50 pages of narrative for my Comprehensive Exam. Not one less; not one more: Fifty, exactly. Not a line more; not a line less. Prior to receiving my questions, I had to submit a goal statement where I talk about my educational and professional goals, as well as my personal, professional, and academic histories. Among other things, I had written about my past involvement as a crisis intervention counselor, and also about my Son's recent death. In the introductory paragraph, I wrote:

> *"I was originally scheduled to begin my comprehensive exams in January, 2009, and was, if fact, enrolled and participating in the first week of HS9919, when my Son, Adam, was killed on January 8, 2009. I have taken the last few months to begin the long, painful process of grief and recovery, but feel compelled to resume my academic journey. Frankly, if I were to wait until I was entirely 'ready and recovered,' I probably would never begin again. No horrible experience compares to the loss of a child to violence. Ironically, approximately a week prior to Adam's death, I was discussing this type of loss with a colleague who told me, 'When your parents die, you're an 'orphan. When your spouse dies, you're a 'widow' or 'widower. But when your child dies, there is no word for that."*

Couldn't have made it clearer, right? Helen Keller would have picked up on the fact that an academic question about grief and death of a loved one might be a bit too close to home, and just might evoke an emotionally-charged response, rather than an intellectual one. You got the part about my kid dying, right?

Now, I've avoided any situations where I might start crying like a blithering idiot in public, to the extent of taking a dollar-an-hour cut in pay at a second job I was working, to keep from talking to people about their kids and their kids' grades. So, I got my Comprehensive Exam questions emailed to me, and guess what the third question was? You guessed it:

> *"Bereaved individuals experience variability in their reactions as they transition to a life without their loved one (Riley, LaMontagne, Hepworth, & Murphy, 2007). Describe three theories used to explain the grief process. Evaluate the efficacy of each theory related to helping a client grieve the loss of a significant person in his/her life. Include strengths and weaknesses of each theory in your discussion."*

Oh, and the *Riley, LaMontagne, Hepworth, & Murphy, 2007* article they gave as a primary reference is entitled, *"Parental Grief Responses and Personal Growth Following the Death of a Child."* Can you say, *"Bad timing?"* How about, *"Faux pas?"* I knew ya could! For some reason, I got the sneaking suspicion that my Comps Exam Mentor didn't read the opening paragraph of my goal statement, and went straight to the education and professional experience parts of my *"bio."* By the way, Adam would have thought the whole thing was hilarious. I certainly didn't at the time, but now, eleven years later, my sense of humor has been restored, and I find the event to be absolutely hilarious. Timing, after all, really *is* everything, when it comes to grief and comedy.

Now, fellow Surviving Parents, I'm not making light of your loss or mine. I realize that the death of my Son is not a laughing matter. And, certainly, the death of your child is not, either. This book is intended to be extremely serious, to deal with the most horrible of tragedies, while using humor to make this bitter topic somewhat palatable. I DON'T believe that God is a practical joker, let alone a cruel one; but I DO believe that he has an incredible sense of humor; and that, in fact, His Divine Sense of Humor is a core component of His Divine Nature, that He instilled in us when He created us in His Image.

Have you ever asked yourself, *"Exactly what does it mean to be 'Created in the Image of God?' I mean, do we physically look like Him*? (I hope not!) *Does God get zits? Does He go to the bathroom?"* Physical and physiological attributes have absolutely nothing to do with the concept of being *"created in His Image."* So, what does? I believe that the traits inherent to being created *"in the Image of God"* are directly linked to emulation of God's Character and His Psychology.

God's Sense-of-Humor has very little, if anything, to do with our ability to make someone laugh; it's about our own ability to see the light of humor in the middle of the darkness of adversity. It's not about being a comedian, it's a way of looking at the world and its problems seriously, while also not taking ourselves too seriously, and helps us to emotionally and spiritually survive. His humor is a reminder that he is with us, even in the darkness.

Many of the aforementioned traits we find in *"God's Nature"* are vitally important in the effective recovery of various forms of trauma and loss. Those traits include, but are not limited to, the desire to know God, to feel compassion and mercy, to exercise forgiveness, loyalty, integrity, morality, conscience, empathy, creativity, faith, trust, hope, joy, appreciation of fun and play, and the innate drive to survive, to be free, to be healthy, and to serve others. And…to have a sense of humor, just like God has.

Those traits, values, and tendencies did not just pop up in a vacuum. They are born out of our life's sometimes-tragic experiences, and our most-significant relationships. *"Sense of humor,"* in acute, sustained stress and grief responses, is emblematic of the finer-tuned qualities of God's Nature, and our own human and divine natures. It can easily be suppressed, or even permanently conditioned out of us by maladaptive effects brought about by Complicated Grief.

"Wait a minute," you ask, *"Are you saying that when God created us in His Image, He gave us a sense of humor? So.....God has a sense of humor???!!"* Of course, He does! If you doubt that, just take a closer look at a platypus. That crazy-looking animal looks like it was put together by a political committee, then voted on by Congress. Or, better still, read some of the most rollickingly-hilarious stories in the Bible, such as Balaam and the Donkey, for example. Believe me: it's cool to look for God's Humor while we are reverently reading the Bible. It gives us a glimpse into a commonly-overlooked facet of the *"Face of God."*

Our sense of humor is one of the most vital gifts that God gives us to survive emotionally, spiritually, and even physically… and to find wonder and joy in a sometimes-terrible world. It is a key *"survival mechanism."* And yet, when we suffer a devastating loss such as losing a child, our sense of humor, and our capacity for joy and hope, happen to be the *"first things to go."*

By the way, I also personally believe that God, more than anyone, totally understands what I have gone through: *BECAUSE*

SOMEONE KILLED HIS KID, TOO. This isn't the first time I've realized the importance of humor in emotional survival. As a former police Detective who investigated crimes against children, and Director of the *Department of Crimes Against Children* and the *National Youth Crisis Hotline* for *Children's Rights of America, Inc.* I long ago learned that the topics I was teaching to law enforcement officers were so despicably painful to talk about, that it was important to make the presentation tolerable, palatable, and something the people would be able to listen to. And, yes, police officers and paramedics, more than anyone, are prone to develop *"gallows humor"* in order to survive. I'm not talking about that macabre form of humor. That's a separate topic.

I'm reminded of the suicide-by-gunshot of a young, college-aged woman in the early 1980's, in a city in the Oklahoma City metroplex. An 18-year-old girl, who had blown her own head off with a handgun. This particular death was notable, because the female victim chose a firearm to kill herself, with the gun being placed in her mouth...which is fairly uncommon in female suicides. However, this case is particularly memorable to me, because, when the veteran Detective processing the crime scene began taking pictures, he noticed a stuffed animal --a basset hound-- set in the corner. I knew the Detective, who later told me his account of what happened at the crime scene. He was, by the way, an excellent investigator, with an impeccable professional reputation.

He told me that the dog looked so sad. On impulse, he picked up the stuffed animal, put it on the body of the dead girl, and took a picture of it with his Polaroid camera, just as the girl's sister entered the room. You see, the police officer who was assigned to guarding the outer perimeter of the crime scene had gone to his squad car for a moment, and the sister slipped past the *"Crime Scene"* tape, and entered the apartment, without having been told what had happened. Needless to say, it was a tragic scene; and the outcome was devastating. The ramifications of that event are obvious; the Detective got into some trouble, but his career survived.

Obviously, putting a sad-looking stuffed dog with tears in his eyes on top of a suicide victim was certainly not appropriate…far from it; nor was taking a picture of it, in the midst of taking crime scene photographs. At the time, it was not seen for what it most-likely was: a psychologically-desperate act which came out of the emotional defenses necessary to deal with the carnage of the world on a daily basis, and that sad and horrendous case, in particular. It was, ultimately, an acute grief and stress response. It was seen as *"conduct unbecoming of an officer."* The Detective was a victim of bad timing, but also a victim of having seen one too many senseless tragedies in his career. His *"gallows humor"* was probably, in my opinion, a subconscious attempt to emotionally survive that terrible moment.

Gallows humor isn't the same as the sense of humor I'm talking about: the kind that allows us to see something humorous in an otherwise bland, uninteresting, or difficult existence. I'm talking about the humor in Bible stories that most people don't pick up on. Jesus has a sense of humor, just like his Heavenly Dad…in fact, He has a terrific one.

"Joel Johnson," you may be thinking, *"How in the world*

can you joke after all you've experienced and seen?" That's a good question, because, as I said previously, to add insult to injury, grieving isn't funny. Since Adam's death, I've managed to avoid developing what therapists refer to as *"Complicated Grief,"* by exercising some key principles of recovery that I have found to be effective and life-saving. I write about them; I teach them; but most importantly, I try to daily live by them. Some of those principles I practice better than others. (For example, for years, I pretty much earned a D-minus in the *"exercise and eat right"* part of taking care of myself, but I'm now finally working on it). One of the most important tools I employ is my sense of humor. It has saved my life. Sense of humor, to me, is serious business. Why?

A key symptom of Complicated Grief among Surviving Parents is a sustained loss of a once-keen sense of humor, as well as a capacity for joy and hope. As a God-given coping mechanism, our sense of humor helps us to survive, as we look at the sometimes terrible world around us. When providing mutual aid support to a parent who has lost a child, one of the tell-tale signs I look for in evaluating whether or not a Surviving Parent is going through Complicated Grief, is the sustained impairment of what once was a keen sense of humor in that individual.

Complicated Grief surpasses the normal, healthy grief and bereavement process, and involves manifestation of some problematic signs and symptoms calling for clinical intervention. It often looks a lot like a combination of post-traumatic stress disorder and clinical depression. I don't want to get into the complicated grief issue too much more at this point, but I do want to ensure we are all on the same page as far as what it means, and what its implications are for our lives.

Here's what I've come to realize in the last eleven years of first-hand experience in the parental grieving process: That effective treatment of trauma and catastrophic loss MUST address the complete human persona in order to be truly effective. I believe that our survival involves an acquirable, holistic skill-set which addresses the whole person. In the grief recovery process, focus must be on cognitive, emotional, psychological, spiritual, physical, behavioral, social, and family-relationship needs. The profound effect that grief --especially Complicated Grief-- has on us cannot and must not be underestimated or disregarded. Our survival as Surviving Parents depends upon it.

I also believe that successful transition from being **victimized** → **to surviving** →**to overcoming** →**to thriving** -→**to conquering** involves the reestablishment and refinement of those human and Divine traits, through training and conditioning, rather than solely through *"talk therapies." "Taking care of ourselves"* involves more than eating and exercising. It must involve the re-introduction of fun. A keen sense of humor can't just be voluntarily turned back on once it has shut down...but it can be nurtured and restored. I believe that sense of humor is not just something we feel; it's something we do.

Elsewhere in this book, I talk about my favorite recreational pass-time: *"mental hot feet,"* which George Carlin described as *"doing something that is so bizarre, it's sure to allow you to 'rent free space' in the head of a total stranger who won't find what you do as funny; just hauntingly puzzling."* Mental Hot Feet are therapeutic exercises for me (See Chapter Thirteen). They are harmless, and make for excellent story telling on Facebook. They also cost little-to-nothing financially, can be done virtually anywhere, and require only the ability and willingness to *"recognize the ridiculous"* around us. They require a keen sense of observation, and situational awareness, in order to spot perfect opportunities to confound people. I've found Mental Hot Feet to be an effective way to self-evaluate; to see how I'm doing.

Again, as I mentioned before, I'm not talking about the aforementioned *"gallows humor"* or *"cop humor,"* which is sometimes, in and of itself, a maladaptive way of coping with the extraordinarily horrible nature of what we're exposed to. *"Cop humor"* involves joking about things that practically any other person would be horrified by, in order to insulate one's self, and to make it possible to function. Over time, it can take its toll, and may be accompanied by many problems commonly associated with PTSD, vicarious traumatization, compassionate fatigue, and/or burnout: four of the most common forms of occupational stress disorders among *"professional heroes, helpers, and healers."* When I hear *"cop humor"* expressed, my natural tendency is to look closer to see if there are other problematic symptoms going on in the individual.

I said it before; I'll say it again: As any successful stand-up comedian will tell you, timing is everything. There are appropriate times to outwardly express our sense of humor, and times when it is possibly not appropriate, due to the needs and conditions of others around us. Nevertheless, sense of humor may play an important role in our own reaction to adversity and loss, even when only-intrinsically applied and practiced. A common risk of this type of adaptive coping mechanism is being misunderstood by others, or even angering them. Also, what I'm talking about is quite different from outbursts of inappropriate joking during times of cataclysmic stress, which is oft a sign of a stress-related adjustment response.

However, in the context of how I believe God wishes for us to utilize the Divine Gift of sense of humor, its employment is vital to our emotional, psychological, physical, and spiritual health. I have a *"Facebook friend"* who, along with her family, experienced an extraordinarily tragic and earth-shaking loss a little over a few years ago: the worst form of loss a family can experience in their lifetime. One of the things that I love most about my friend is also one of the most promising aspects of her personality...a key indicator to me that she shows great hope of surviving, thriving, overcoming, and conquering. I'm talking about her sense of humor.

While she will never *"get over"* her loss, I pray she and her family will eventually integrate their horrible loss into their lives...not to *"get past it,"* but to *"get through it."* They have an incredible relationship, lots of support from family and friends, and the tools they need to make it through what they are going through. I admire them very much, and my heart is broken over their loss. I personally believe that my friend's sense of humor will continue to play an important part in her healing process, and that her example will keep her family close to one another. God has given her, as he has given all of us, many, many precious gifts, many of which are vitally important as *"Survival Mechanisms."* Of all of them, Sense of Humor is one of the most Glorious!

Chapter Four

"God," "God's Will," **and other Debate Topics**

Over the last decade, in my many religious and spiritual discussions with Surviving Parents and other suffering loved ones, I've found that --among those who believe in some concept of God-- their opinions of God's Nature and Personality vary greatly. Further exploring that, I've come to believe that Believers' perceptions of God often tend to be remarkably similar to the image that they hold of their own earthly, human parents. Some opinions of God's Character are that He is either:

- *"The Ultimate Ward Cleaver:"* an Even-Tempered, Patient, Consistent, Long-suffering, and Faithful Father and Dad who is Everywhere; All-Knowing, Wise, Just, Patient, Long-suffering, Loving, Understanding, Compassionate, Trustworthy, Firm, Fair, and Always There…and Someone Who Keeps His Promises; or,

- *"Disney World Dad:"* lavishing gifts and treats upon His children during visitation, but not always there when the trouble starts; or,

- *"Mr. No Nonsense:"* a powerful, distant, and non-compromising Father who expects absolute obedience, and who requires full submission and adherence to a clear set of rules, standards, and laws; or,

- *"Mr. Popularity:"* a permissive Divine Parent who allows His (or Her) children to do whatever they want to, regardless of the consequences to them; or,

- *"Mr. Not Around:"* an Absentee Parent who is sometimes, rarely, or never there, and can't really be relied upon; or,
- *"Mr. Harvey Milquetoast:"* an ineffectual, powerless parent, who doesn't have the faculties, strengths, or capability to take care of, or protect, His children; or,
- *"The Joker:"* A cruel trickster and prankster, who is emotionally abusive, and who tends to give nice things to His children, then yank them away at inopportune times; or,
- *"The Riddler:"* who delights in confounding his children with *"mysteries;"* or,
- *"The Bad Guy:"* an abusive parent who has inflicted hardship and tragedy upon them; or,
- *"Mr. Magoo:"* who is blind to what is occurring in the lives of His children; or,
- *"The Coward:"* an abandoning parent who left home long ago, with no regard for how that abandonment would devastate his children; or,
- *"Casper, the Friendly Ghost:"* an imaginary figment.

I have often found that Surviving Parents, and other grieving loved ones --who believe in God-- have various views of whether or not anything and everything exists or occurs outside of God's Will. Oft times, their belief comes from something they heard their Pastor or Bible Study Leader say, rather than seriously exploring the Word of God on their own. Some believe that nothing happens that God either doesn't make happen or actively permits to happen. This false belief is often fostered by statements by religious, well-meaning types, who attempt to offer advice, help, and counsel by saying things such as, *"We can't always understand God's Will for our lives;" "Well, the Lord giveth and the Lord taketh away;" "We must believe and be comforted by knowing that it was God's Perfect Will,"* et cetera.

Regardless of whether or not the theologians, pastoral counselors, and well-intended friends who make these types of statements to Surviving Parents are correct or incorrect in their theology; I believe that their well-intended statements may, in certain cases, exacerbate the suffering of those people, as well as magnifying the pre-existing animosity which is already being directed toward God...thus making it less likely that those individuals will ever feel comfortable seeking out help from God, or his earthly representatives...when they need it the most.

It has been my experience that Surviving Parents often tend to develop animosity toward God at some point in the grieving process, because they assume that in the death of their child, God was either a complicit co-conspirator, or perpetrator, or a neglectful witness who knew it was going to happen, saw it happen, but stood by and didn't do anything to prevent it from happening. I don't know about you, but if I held any of those views, *I'd* be angry, too.

Many years ago, a grief and bereavement expert named Elizabeth Kubler-Ross wrote about what she originally referred to as the *"Five Stages of Grief,"* associated with the process of dying. Those five stages are *"Denial, Anger, Bargaining,*

Depression, and Acceptance." Incidentally, in her later years, Ms. Kubler-Ross announced publicly that, if she had it to do all over again, she would not have called those states *"Stages,"* because, as it turns out, they aren't clear-cut processes moving from one to the next; but were rather more fluid, interruptive, and flexible than she had originally described.

Years later, another grief and bereavement expert named Ken Moses described a process that I believe is more accurate: that while grieving, the sufferer's various emotional and psychological states are much more like the ocean tide, ebbing and flowing, toward and away from the shore; and that there is often an *"undertow"* lying beneath the surface, opposite of the surface ebb and flow, which is prone to sweep our feet out from under us when we least expect it.

To use the *"tide"* metaphor: have you ever gone to the beach, waded out into the surf, to find yourself about waist-to chest-deep in water? You may have experienced the tide pushing you in one direction on the surface, when suddenly, the undertow grabs your feet out from under you, in the opposite direction of the surface tide. If you don't know it's coming, that response can be surprising, disorienting, and distressing. Grief is much like that. You may find yourself moving along in one direction (emotionally), then all of a sudden feeling your feet ripped out from under you, causing you to topple backward.

I have often described this maddening process like this: imagine that you are required to walk down a sidewalk every day, and around a corner onto an intersecting street. Each day you turn that corner, one of two things happens: either a friend is there to greet you, give you a hug and a $100 bill…or an enemy is there, who will promptly and consistently kick you in the gut. You never know which one you're going to encounter, but you are required to daily come around that corner, anyway.

That is precisely what I have experienced, many times, when I have encountered a reminder of Adam. I may find myself crying for joy, smiling, feeling warm and comforted…or immediately feeling sad, forlorn, nauseous, and depressed. Not knowing what I will be feeling from one time to the next is maddening, and sometimes even makes me angry at myself.

Anger is a normal part of the grieving process. It may manifest in many different ways, and may or may not be directed toward self, other people, our deceased loved one, or even God. Since people tend to have their own unique opinions or beliefs about God's role in the death of their child, it is only natural that they may entertain the possibility that God either took their child from them (like He is some sort of Trickster, or that he loves to snatch gifts away from us after bestowing them upon us), or that He had some mysterious, divine, self-serving reason for taking their child, while dooming us to lifelong suffering.

Other prospects include that God was not concerned enough about the impact of their loss to prevent Him from going ahead with his *"Plan,"* that He was powerless over the tragic events, and *"wasn't there for them."* Surviving Parents embracing those views may therefore be angry at Him because of His assumed impotence. Other people acquire the belief that a Loving God would not do something like that to them, and therefore, because the loss happened, God must not exist at all.

Then they sometimes foster anger toward themselves for believing in a fairy tale, or remain angry at someone who does not exist.

Again, for whatever reason, anger at God during and after a catastrophic loss is often connected to a belief that God either orchestrated the death of their child, was complicit in that death, or was either uncaring enough, or incapable of preventing it. These beliefs are often linked to a false belief that nothing happens outside of the God's Will; that we can't always understand God's Divine Will; that God's Divine Will is a mystery, and is not for us to second-guess; and that God is perfectly happy when we suffer a loss, because His Plan worked out. Also, to add further insult to injury, this false belief also suggests that we are totally out of line by questioning, being disgruntled with, or not accepting our loss as being *"God's Divine Will."*

I don't believe that it is EVER *"God's Will"* that a child be raped, tortured, or murdered. I don't believe that it is EVER *"God's Will"* that other obscene atrocities are committed by one human being against another. When *"Free Will"* was spun into motion, it created a situation in which people had the freedom to say *"No,"* and to sin against God. Rebellion is possible, so that obedience to God can have meaning and value. If we were incapable of rejecting God, then accepting God into our lives would have no value or credence. If we were puppets on strings, our actions could not be attributed to our loyalty to the puppeteer, but rather to He who pulls the strings.

My Grandmother, Frances Hopson: *"My Mammaw,"* died in her sleep at the age of 101; prematurely, I might add. When she was 90, she quit climbing the June apple tree in her front yard, because she outlived the tree. She suffered a series of strokes in the years prior to her death in 1995. Adam was only six years old when my Mammaw had her first major stroke. He never got the opportunity to know how wonderful she was, except through the many stories I told him about her. He didn't know her like I knew her. But now he does. His mansion is two doors down from hers, on their very own *"Street of Gold."* I'll bet she invites him over for cookies and cocoa, and an occasional *"sleepover."*

After her last stroke, my Mammaw was sometimes lucid, but usually totally *"out of it,"* believing she was a young girl, *"back on the farm,"* outside of White Oak, Oklahoma. Prior to her last stroke, she had been sharp as a tack and independent. After that fateful day, was miserable, debilitated, and only a shell of the wonderful person she had always been. But, while my Mammaw usually didn't know where she was, she ALWAYS knew who I was: Her *"Pepper"* (my childhood nickname). She loved me more than life itself. She put me through college, and was devoted to me my entire life. When my Mammaw closed her eyes for the last time, and took her last breath, she passed away. I was relieved that she had finally found peace, and was free from suffering. Adam, on the other hand, did not pass away. That's nonsense. Adam was killed. Not murdered, though he was the victim of homicide, yet it was determined to be *"justifiable homicide."* Not only do I believe that; I accept that.

Adam died as a result of a tragic string of events, all involving Free Will on the part of several well-intended people, including Adam. It is my belief that his death was not God's Will, yet he died. God desired that Adam live a long, full life, and to

69

continue to help people. He desired that Adam be free from the pain, suffering, and difficulties of mental illness and substance abuse. God's desires, however, were superseded by Free Will. Adam's death was not a good thing, in and of itself, but, in spite of that, God had made him a promise two thousand years before he was born: that:

"for those who love God, all things work together for good, for those who are called according to his purpose" (**Romans 8:28 - ESV**).

That promise isn't for everyone, but it certainly was for Adam, because Adam loved God, and was called according to God's Purpose. So, his death is working together with a multitude of other events, even to this day, to bring about God's Will; and that's good.

I'm confident that God did not snatch him away. I know in my heart that Father God and the Lord Jesus Graciously Received him, early that cold, dark morning, on Thursday, January 8, 2009. I'm equally confident that one of the first people to greet him when he arrived in Heaven was my Mammaw. Every single time I have been asked the question of whether or not I was personally angry at God for Adam's death, my response has been based upon soul-searching honesty, and deep reflection: I cannot recall one single micro-second, since the early morning of January 8, 2009, to this present moment, when I have been angry at God for my loss. In fact, I figure that, if there is anyone who can truly empathize, understand, and comprehend the enormity, uniqueness, and terrible nature of my sense of loss, it is God.

Why? Because He has gone through what I have been through.
You see…

Someone Killed His Kid, Too

The music died the tragic day
Three bullets took my Son away.
The light went out; the dark was born
The day I learned to grieve and mourn.

Before that day, I thought I knew
What grieving parents suffer through.
But, that great loss could not compare
To any pain that I could share.

My heart became an empty place;
My joy was gone, without a trace.
I thought that peace could only lie
In hope that I would one day die.

But then it came: It was so odd,
That I was not at odds with God,
Because He understood, and knew.
You see, someone killed *His* Kid, too.

He could have spared Himself the loss
When Jesus hung upon the Cross.
He could have made all time stand still,
If He'd suspended Man's free will.

He could have struck the evil down,
Removed the thorns, and placed a crown
On Jesus' head, and made a slave
Of sinful men He died to save.

And yet, He chose that day to give
His Son, so we could one day live
With Him in Glorious Paradise.
He gave for us a Precious Price.

So, on my knees, I do not pray
For Him to take the pain away,
But, for the strength to daily choose
To give my pain for Him to use.

I gave my loss, my broken will,
My gifts and skills, so He could fill
Those broken hearts, and wipe the tears,
And soothe the pain, and quash the fears

Of those who weep, and need to share
The horrid pain that can't compare
To any other kind of grief:
The kind that offers no relief.

He did not take my Son away;
Now in His Love, I choose to stay,

Because I know He did receive
My Son, I now choose to believe

That one day, I'll be whole again;
My broken heart, my God will mend.
His Gentle Hand will wipe away
All tears, and I'll forever stay

With my Son in a Land of Grace
And Peace. I know God will erase
All mem'ries of my loss and pain,
And in His Home, I shall remain.

For now, I give the emptiness
To God, so He can heal and bless
The hearts of other parents, while
They grieve the loss of their own child.

This simple truth that makes us whole,
That soothes our most-ravaged soul:
That when we don't know how to pray,
God's Grace will always let us stay

Inside His Love, safe in His Heart;
And from our lives He won't depart.
He'll stay beside us as we grieve,
If we will trust Him and believe.

But that is easier said than done
For folks like me who've lost a Son.
My Friends, commit to play a part
In helping God heal broken hearts.

The music died that tragic day
Three bullets took my Son away.
For now, I hear the faintest sound;
One Day the Music Will Abound.

The Lesson of Claudia's Spaghetti Sauce

God speaks to me through many things; some are pretty weird. I have heard him speak to me through everything from a Scripture verse to a plate of spaghetti. Suffice it to say, I generally learn more from the Word than from the food. And, what I have also come to understand is, we sometimes learn later, after meditating for a while. We get the instant message, then later, the hidden, deeper, truer message from things we take into our minds, hearts, and our bodies. One example of this is a lesson I learned from *"Claudia's Spaghetti Sauce."* Through it, I came to better understand Roman's 8:28 (ESV):

"And we know that for those who love God, all things work together for good, for those who are called according to His Purpose."

Back in the late 1980's, after Debbie and I separated, I returned to my home church: First Indian Rocks Baptist Church, in Largo, FL. I became close friends with a guy in the Adult Singles class, who remodeled offices and restaurants for a living. One of his masterpieces was an Italian restaurant in Bellaire Bluffs, FL. As a barter arrangement, he had remodeled the restaurant in return for free food for life! The owner of the restaurant was a man named *"Claudia."* In addition to feeding my friend, he also bestowed a huge lot of coupons to him, good for free meals for his friends and companions. Rules: There was a limit as to how many of those coupons he could use each month, and that recipients had to be in the company of my friend.

One of Claudia's specialties was his spaghetti sauce, made

from a recipe that Claudia kept a closely guarded secret. As a tradition, following a meal, my friend and I would always go back to the kitchen to pay our compliments to the Chef, and to thank him for the feast. On one particular evening, I asked Claudia if he would give me the recipe to his spaghetti sauce; he delicately refused. A few weeks later, my friend and I walked back into the kitchen, and saw several bowls filled with various ingredients, and a large mixing bowl, on top of a metal table in the center of the room.

I walked over to view the contents of the bowls, and saw things like chopped tomatoes, tomato puree, diced onion, minced garlic, chopped green pepper, and water. I recognized almost all the ingredients, because they were what I put in my own tasty, but not record-breaking, spaghetti sauce. As I looked closer, though, I saw one single bowl with a black paste in it. I called out Claudia's name, and when he looked at me, I pointed to that particular bowl, got a sly, Cheshire-Cat grin on my face, and said, *"Oh, Claudia, what's this?"* (pointing to the bowl). Claudia's grin matched mine as he replied, *"That's it."*

However, with no matter how much I coaxed, Claudia would not tell me what it was. Not to be thwarted, when Claudia turned his back, I quickly stuck a fingertip into the black goo, and put it to my tongue. I figured that, even if I did not recognize the flavor, I could remember it, and go to an herb store I knew of, to try to find out what this mysterious ingredient was.

What occurred in the following moments cannot possibly compare to any culinary experience I had ever had, except when I chomped down on a fried chicken liver in Grandy's, and found out the hard way that a gall bladder was still attached to the liver, under the breading. It tasted like a *"pus bomb"* had just gone in my mouth; it was horrible! No amount of water or milk could ease the impact of that horrible flavor, for the next few minutes.

As I spat out the black stuff into my hand, said some less-than-complimentary things, went over to a nearby sink and cupped water into my hand and into my mouth, spitting it out into the sink. I turned around to spy Claudia and my friend laughing their heads off. Of course, Claudia again refused to reveal his secret. In fact, I never found out what the secret ingredient was. Now, I realize that if you prepared spaghetti sauce from everything else that remained on the table, you would have...Ragu: Tasty, but nothing to write home about. The black stuff, in and of itself, was putrid. It would have to be mixed carefully, in what would probably be a very small amount, for it to transform Claudia's sauce into a masterpiece.

I also recognize that even if you included it, you would also have to know just when and how much of the ingredient to drop into the mixing bowl. Only Claudia, the Master Chef, knew all the secrets to his sauce. I must say that I have looked at many recipes, trying to figure out what that black garbage was. Its exact nature and origin elude me to this day. I might add that I have never again been tempted to put an unidentified object or substance into my mouth!

A few days later, I was sitting in the waiting room of a tire store, thinking of that experience, and laughing at myself. All of a sudden, it occurred to me that it was a perfect analogy to explain the intricacies of Romans 8:28. You see, not all things in the world are good. Some are dark and horrid, like that unknown herb. Not all things work for good. The black stuff was horrible, and if the wrong amount had been dropped into the bowl at the wrong time, it could have ruined the sauce, rather than making it a culinary marvel. Also, only Claudia knew how and when to add it to the ingredient mix. For all I knew, that black stuff might have been added when the sauce was cold, or when it was heated up.

In this obvious metaphor, God is the Master Chef. Some things, which are clearly (to me) NOT within the realm of what is part of HIS Will, such as rape and murder of a child, are intended by the Enemy to destroy us. They are, in and of themselves, certainly not good. However, God, the Ultimate Master Chef, is capable of utilizing our darkest life's experiences, to work together with other experiences, to fulfill HIS Will, to glorify Himself, and to bring to us healing, recovery, and victory.

That is particularly important to understand when you realize that Satan created --and dropped in-- the putrid black stuff into our lives. In spite of Satan's shrewdest schemes, however, God is infinitely more powerful, wise, knowledgeable, and capable than *"Split Foot"* is, and has a miraculous knack of turning dark defeat into Glorious Victory, if we will only let Him.

Oh, and by the way, I believe it is important to point out that Romans 8:28 does not put itself out there as a Universal Promise to everyone. It says that ALL things work TOGETHER for GOOD, for THOSE WHO LOVE GOD, and are CALLED ACCORDING TO HIS PURPOSE. It may or may not apply to others. I'm not saying it can't be true for any person...just that God did not utter that Promise to anyone at that particular time, other than His Children, called by Him.

Whether or not a person loves God and is truly called, is, of course, not for any of us to say. It is ultimately between God and that individual. However, I can say with confidence, that, after careful examination of the evidence of Adam's life, there is no doubt in my mind that the verse was intended for him, and for me. While Adam and I were fallible and flawed human beings (and I still am), we definitely love God, and are called by Him.

Chapter Five

There's No Single Word for What I Am Now

To repeat what I said at the beginning of this book: Someone, somewhere, once said, *"If your parents die, you're an 'orphan;' if your spouse dies, you're a 'widow' or a 'widower.' But if your child dies, there's no word for that."* True.

There's no single word in the English language to describe who or what I am now; what I became on January 8, 2009. As the father of an *"only child,"* I'm no longer, legally, a Dad. As a 66-year-old man with a vasectomy, it's highly unlikely I'll ever be a Dad again, by natural means, although there are a few young loved ones who call me *"Dad,"* and who have asked Barb and me to be their *"Surrogate Parents."*

It's hard to explain sometimes, but that has been one of the most difficult things to deal with as a grieving ex-parent. It's embedded within the core of my self-pity. I've not only lost the most important person in my Universe; I've lost a major part of me. I no longer feel like a complete person, even though I am much further along now than I was eleven years ago. Why? Nothing was more important to me than the responsibility, duty, joy, privilege, and supreme pleasure associated with the most important job, and most wonderful blessing, God ever gave me: being Adam's Dad.

Adam doesn't need me anymore. He's now totally in the arms of his true, Heavenly Father who loves him so much more than I ever could. He has no more pain, fear, turmoil, troubles, or problems. He's totally at peace, and now experiences everlasting joy. As much as Adam loves me, and enjoyed his time with his

Dad, I realize that nothing I could ever say to him could possibly coax him into returning back to earth to be with me. I also know that one day I'll be with him again, and that our relationship will be different, but perfect, as we sit together at the feet of Jesus.

Nevertheless, it still hurts. Sometimes I still feel so empty and alone. The ache is terrible. It hits me sometimes like a swift, unexpected kick in the gut. I'll be supposedly doing fine, then…WHAM! I feel like doubling over, and I just want to cry. I feel so guilty sometimes, as I remember times and opportunities that I should have or could have done more for him, or when I disappointed myself in the job I was doing as a parent.

My mistakes are ever before me, but thankfully, so is the beauty and wonder of our relationship…our special friendship…and the understanding and mutual respect and admiration that Adam and I had for each other. As much as I love my wife, my best friends, and my family, I must confess that I was never closer to anyone in the world than I was to Adam.

I thank God for several things, though: for the time I did have with Adam…at least, for the time I didn't waste. I thank Him for the last day I spent with Adam in person…how wonderful it was, and that we got to play a duet together that day at Living Waters Church in Bentonville, AR. Ironically, the Song we played was a composition Adam wrote of *"Jesus Loves Me."* It's so ironic that the very first Song Adam learned as a baby, his mother's nightly lullaby to him, was the last Song we would play together.

I thank God that, however brief it was, our last phone conversation, on Monday evening, January 5, 2009, was fun, funny, pleasant, and that Adam was in good cheer, bright, and hopeful. We talked about how well he was doing, how the tips were very good at his pizza delivery job, and how he was looking forward to going on to college in the fall…to eventually become a lawyer. Adam wanted to champion the helpless and vulnerable people of this world, who could not protect themselves. He wanted his life to be significant. He didn't think it was. He couldn't have been more mistaken, though…as you'll see in the later chapters of this book.

I thank God that I can't recall a single conversation that I ever had with Adam, no matter how brief, in which I didn't tell him that I loved him. I used to ask him, speaking in third person: *"Buddy, does your Dad say he loves you too much?"* Adam would grin and say, *"No, Dad. It's cool."* I thank God that our last talk was not harsh. We had so very few arguments throughout his entire life. In fact, I can recall only one. Since his death, I've talked to so many parents who feel guilt over the fact that their last words to their dead child were argumentative or harsh. To those parents, I have some things to offer you in Chapter Twenty-Eight, which I hope will be helpful to you, and will help you to heal.

I thank God for the four phone messages that I had saved over the last two years prior to his death: messages from Adam. Each day I get to hear his voice. I hear the love and devotion that he had for me. I hear him speaking of *"some great ideas"* that he'd been having, which were, in fact, about his *"Battle Cry"* for Christians, which can be found in Chapter Sixteen. Reading Adam's own words, written in his Journal, where he described his past struggle with his beliefs, and his affirmation of his faith in

Jesus, I especially thank God that I can KNOW with assurance that my Son didn't die alone, and that I know where he is now.

I can't imagine how horrible it would feel to not know that, yet I know that there are so many parents out there who have that fear and pain to deal with, on top of their catastrophic loss. To those parents, I hope that some things I have to share with you in this book will give you comfort. Please read Chapter Twenty-Eight…jump ahead and read it now, if you feel the need to.

Chapter Six

The Day We Brought Adam Home, *"Right Out of the Crate"*

My first wife, Debbie --Adam's Mom-- and I were married June 14, 1975. More than anything, we wanted to be parents. However, for medical reasons, we were not able to produce a biological child. We decided to adopt a baby, and entered into the extremely complicated and arduous process of being approved as adoptive parents. I was serving as a Detective with the Norman Police Department, and Deb --a Registered Nurse-- was employed as Director of Nursing for a convalescent facility in Shawnee, OK. During that time, I was working closely with a Professor at the University of Oklahoma, Dr. Sara Nixon.

Being aware that Deb and I were wanting to adopt, one day Sara called me and told me that she knew a young woman who was pregnant, who wished to give up her child for adoption to a Christian family. We knew her identity, but did not know her personally. Andrea, Adam's birth mother, was a young student at Oklahoma Baptist University, my first college alma mater. She had gotten pregnant with Adam's birth father, who did not want to be a parent at the time. Andrea concealed the pregnancy from him until she was far enough along to prohibit an abortion. She had been afraid that Adam's birth father would try to pressure her to terminate the pregnancy. Dr. Nixon was a friend of her family, and told her about Deb and me. She facilitated our indirect contact with Andrea through an attorney in Norman. We began the process of being approved for private adoption, and, a few months later, were granted permission to adopt.

I remember exactly where I was on July 31, 1984, when I was notified that our baby boy had come into this world: I was interviewing a sexual assault victim at the Norman Municipal Hospital Emergency Room, when I received a message from the Police Dispatcher that I had an urgent phone call. As soon as I could, I returned the call, and was told that I was the father of a brand-spanking new, absolutely-perfect, baby boy. Deb and I had already decided on our Son's name: Adam Joshua Johnson. When I returned to my police vehicle, I got on the radio, went *"10-8,"* (back in service), and announced to my co-workers that *"Adam Joshua Johnson is 10-97"* (meaning that he had arrived).

To say we were excited and filled with joy is a gross understatement! But, at the same time, we were scared to death, due to the fact that birth parents have a right to change their mind within 48 hours of a baby's birth. We feared that the first time Andrea held little Adam in her arms, and looked into his beautiful eyes, that she would find it impossible to give him up. By the Grace of God, she did not change her mind, and, two days after the call, we arrived at our attorney's office to meet our Son for the first time. We got to the law offices of Silas Wolf, our attorney, before Adam's arrival. The wait seemed like forever. Deb checked and rechecked the diaper bag at least a half-dozen times, and was locked and loaded with Adam's first bottle of formula, ready to be put in the microwave. He arrived hungry. Boy, did that kid eat! I recall he went through at least two bottles before we left the attorney's office!

I can't even begin to describe the emotions I experienced the first time I held my baby boy in my arms. Relief, joy, excitement --and especially, gratitude-- flooded my heart. At the same time, the stark realization hit me that I was now a father, and that in a split second, my entire world had changed. I was now *"Adam's Dad:"* the most important job responsibility that I would ever have.

The enormity of that sense of responsibility was colossal. I remember exiting the building, as Deb carried our Son out to our yellow Honda Accord, and I placed Adam in his brand-new car seat in the back seat. Deb rode home in the back seat, sitting beside Adam, holding his little hand, talking to him every inch of the way. We got home within a few minutes, and carried Adam into his new home for the very first time.

That night, recalling an epic scene from the television mini-series, *"Roots,"* I took little Adam out into the back yard of our home, held him up to Heaven, high above my head, and dedicated his little life to the Lord. I will never forget the clear summer sky, the bright moon and shining stars, as God smiled down upon us.

Chapter Seven

"Dad, I've Just Got So Many Things Going On"

For three and a half years prior to Adam's birth, I had been working a special undercover assignment, in addition to my standard investigative duties as a Detective. The special assignment involved proactive, covert investigation and apprehension of child pornography collectors and distributors. Shortly after Adam's birth, I received an invitation to join a national organization, headquartered in Clearwater, Florida.

This position would allow me to impact the horrible problems of child abuse and exploitation on a national level, and to assist law enforcement agencies throughout the country in combatting those problems. After much prayer and deliberation, I made the decision to resign from Norman Police Department, and to accept a position as one of the program directors for Children's Rights of America, Inc. a non-profit organization that located and recovered missing and exploited children.

In January, 1985, Debbie and I moved to Clearwater, Florida, but returned to Oklahoma approximately 20 months later, so that Debbie could be near her Mother, who was extremely ill. I took a position as Assistant Chief of Police for the Luther (OK) Police Department, while maintaining my affiliation with Children's Rights of America. Two months after joining the

Luther Police Department, I was promoted to Chief of Police.

Meanwhile, at home, Debbie and I taught Adam to read, well before kindergarten age. It came as no surprise to us that, when evaluated, he scored extremely high, developmentally. In addition to intellect and aptitude, as a pre-schooler, Adam demonstrated that he was well beyond his years in terms of empathy, sense of humor, and insight. Out of nowhere, he would say things that would fill us with surprise, wonder, and pride as a mother and father. A perfect example of this is wrapped within one of my all-time favorite memories of a middle-of-the-night encounter that occurred a few days before his third birthday.

After Debbie and I had returned to Oklahoma from Florida, we encountered some difficulties in our marriage. Debbie had recently shared with me about how unhappy she was, and that she was strongly considering divorcing me. It was a very difficult time for us both. I had much to learn about being a good husband. However, Deb assured me that, in spite of my grave shortcomings as a spouse, I was an excellent father.

We were weighing our options, and had decided to try marital counseling. Early on, we had agreed to never speak in anger or hostility in Adam's presence, and to never say anything negative about each other when talking to him. However, in spite of our best efforts, Adam had sensed that there was something wrong between his Mom and Dad. One pretty clear indicator was that we were now sleeping in separate bedrooms.

One night in July, 1987, I was alone in bed, lying on my right side, wrapped deep in thought about the uncertainty of our marital status. All of a sudden, I got a weird feeling that I was being watched. A moment later, I felt a soft touch on my left shoulder. I rolled over, and looked directly into Adam's eyes, just barely peeking at me over the top of the mattress. As I saw the troubled look on my little boy's face, I asked, *"Honey Bear, is something wrong?"* Adam responded, *"I can't sleep, Dad."* (NOTE: Two of Adam's playmates in Luther were the Son and daughter of a pastor friend of mine. They called their father *"Dad,"* and their mother, *"Mom."* Following in their example, Adam had recently begun calling Debbie and me *"Mom"* and *"Dad,"* instead of *"Mommy"* and *"Daddy,"* because, in his mind, that was what big kids did.)

I responded by asking, *"Why can't you sleep?"* to which he replied, *"I need to talk."* Realizing it must be a matter of paramount importance to my little man, I smiled and said, *"Well, what do you need to talk about..."* ::looking at my watch:: *"at three o'clock in the morning?"* Adam replied, *"Dad, I just have so many things going on."* I had to bite my tongue to keep from laughing out loud in his little face. It was so cute! I looked him in the eye, and said with a serious tone: *"Well, life is just a set of trials and struggles when you're turning three, isn't it, Son?"*

Adam nodded his head silently. Knowing exactly what he wanted to do, I asked, *"Well, Son, do you want Dad to get up so we can talk, or do you want to get up here with me?"* After a moment of quiet contemplation, Adam said, *"I'll just get up there with you."* I helped him climb into bed, roll over onto my right side, and to settle down, facing me. I held out two fingers of my left hand, which Adam grasped immediately with his right hand.

For the next few minutes, we were suspended in time and

space as we gazed into each other's eyes. Rather than talking about what was on his mind, Adam silently held on to my fingers, and after a couple of minutes, he smiled, then closed his eyes, and drifted off to sleep. The moment he dozed off, I began to cry, then to weep, as the full impact of how his little life was being affected by the decision that his Mom and I were about to make. Just then, as Mary --Jesus' mother-- had

"...treasured up all these things, pondering them in her heart" (Luke 2:19 – ESV)

at the time of his birth, I tucked the memory of that magical moment into my own heart...and have never forgotten it.

I have pulled it out to treasure it countless times throughout Adam's life here on earth, and will continue to do so. Sometimes I cry as I recall the sound of his little voice, and the look in his loving eyes. Sometimes I smile; sometimes I laugh out loud. Sometimes my heart is warmed and comforted; sometimes it aches in agony. But regardless of what I am feeling, the moments of recollection are always treasured...because they remind me of how Adam was wise beyond his years, kind, generous, giving, loving, and forgiving.

Each time I think of the brilliance of his wit and intellect; his sense of empathy for others; his strong sense of justice; his raucous, hilarious sense of humor; and his unselfish devotion to making the world a kinder, gentler, more loving place for those who were in pain...I see God, because there is no doubt in my mind that Adam was made in His Image. These insights into Adam's Godly nature are never clearer to me than when I look back on the day I learned about *"The Man with the T-Shirt."*

Chapter Eight

The Man with the T-Shirt

As I mention elsewhere in this book, Adam was a *"Prayer Warrior"* who had a frank, honest, and effective way of talking to God. I knew this, based upon the results that I saw from his prayers…and by his most-private thoughts that he shared in his Journal…unread by me, until after his death. He prayed, and yet, I never heard him pray out loud, once he got the *"Now I lay me down to sleep"* prayer out of his system, when he was a little guy.

Once, when I asked him about why he always praying silently, he said that what he had to say was between him and God. When it came to praying, he was a marathon runner, not a sprinter. If he had something on his heart to pray about, he was faithful to keep praying day after day, week after week….and, as it turned out…year after year. One of the most powerful examples of his faithfulness to keep people and situations that were placed on his heart in prayer was the *"Man with the T-shirt."*

When Adam was seven years old, I drove to Edmond, OK to pick him up, to take him with me on the road for a summer of speaking engagements. We were driving southbound on I-35, south of Purcell, OK, when it occurred to me that he was being unusually quiet. I looked over and saw that he was about to cry. I immediately pulled over onto the shoulder of the highway, and asked him what was wrong. He looked at me, with tears welling up in his beautiful eyes, and said, *"Dad, I saw the world's worst t-shirt."*

I asked him to tell me all about it. He said that, earlier that day, he had seen a man in a mall parking lot in Edmond, who was wearing a t-shirt that said, *"Jesus Knows Diddly."* He then asked me why a man would wear something that would hurt Jesus' feelings. I felt like I had just been hit in the gut, and immediately starting praying silently, asking for God to give me the words to comfort my Son...while also praying that God would take hold of me immediately, and not let me say what I wanted to do to that....I won't use the words I was thinking...*person* who would wear a t-shirt in public that would not only grieve God, but that would also hurt the mind and heart of my precious little boy.

I admit, initially I wanted to track that clown down, and yank him through the keyhole of his car door. But then, I thought of Saul of Tarsus, and how he had zealously persecuted Christians at their executions, no doubt mocking them with scorn as he held the coats of the men who stoned those Believers to death. I thought of the bitterness and hardness of Saul's heart, and how, on that road leading to Damascus, he had encountered Jesus. I told Adam about how cruel and callous Saul was, and how God's love and forgiveness had changed him from Persecutor to Believer.

I shared with my little boy that if we would pray every day for that Man with the T-Shirt, God would speak to him, and give him the opportunity to make the decision that Saul had made on that Damascus Road. We all know the rest of Saul's story, of how Saul became the Apostle Paul. I never heard Adam pray out loud for that man, but I had all the confidence in the world that he did faithfully pray for him.

Six months later, I was talking to Adam on the phone. As was common at the conclusion of our discussions, I asked him if

94

he had any questions for his Dad. After a moment's pause, Adam asked, *"Dad, how will I know when it's all right with God for me to quit praying for that Man with the T-shirt?"* With that single question, my little Prayer Warrior taught me far more than I could ever hope to teach him about prayer, and secretly in my heart, brought me to my knees. You could have knocked me over with a feather, as I sat there, feeling my face begin to burn, as I squeezed a few tears from my eyes.

You see, I must confess that I was not faithful to pray for that man daily, and that after a few weeks, I had forgotten about him altogether...with the exception of an occasional memory of that touching moment on the side of the road, the tearful look in my little boy's eyes, and the trembling of his little lip. His question humbled me, and instilled so much pride in him, while at the same time causing me to feel secret shame for not having been faithful to do what I had encouraged Adam to do. I managed to summon up the presence of mind to tell Adam that if he would ask God, and let Him know that he was more than willing to keep praying for the Man with the T-Shirt, that God would let him know when his prayer had been answered.

I also shared with him about the painting of Jesus standing at the front door of someone's home, knocking. I pointed out to him that the unusual thing about that picture was that there was no doorknob on the outside of the door. The artist seemed to be illustrating that as Jesus knocks on our door, wanting to come in, it is entirely our decision to open the door from the inside to allow Him to enter. I told him that God is patient and long-suffering, but that if we absolutely and finally tell Him to quit knocking and to go away, he is a Gentleman, and will do so.

A few weeks later, Adam told me that God had told him it was okay to stop praying for the Man with the T-shirt. He wasn't sure why, but he absolutely knew that it was okay to cease praying for that man. We talked about how neither of us might ever know the outcome of that prayer. Had the man accepted the Lord, or allowed his heart to be so hardened that God withdrew his invitation? I told Adam that, if the man accepted Jesus, he would get to meet him when he went to Heaven, because Adam's prayers got the man into Heaven.

Chapter Nine

"Dad, I've Got This Friend…"

Posted by me on Facebook, in 2015: *"I had a haunting dream last night...a very different kind of dream than the usual ones I have about my Son, Adam. "Dad, I've got this friend..." are words that I heard on quite a few occasions, when called by Adam...often in the middle of the night. Invariably, he was about to put me on the phone with a friend who was in pain or in trouble. While growing up, when staying with me, Adam had spent countless hours sitting near me as I talked to endangered and hurting children and youth on the National Youth Crisis Hotline. He told me once that he told his friends, "If my Dad can't help you through this, no one can."*

In my dream, Adam came up to me with a little ragamuffin: a long-haired child, who appeared to be about 10 years of age. Adam began to explain to me how the boy needed help...that he had been abused, neglected, and abandoned, and that he needed me to take care of him. Happy to do so, I agreed...but I was haunted by the sense that Adam was somehow not aware that he had been killed six years prior.

In my dream, I felt that I must tell him about how he had died, and asked if I could talk to him in private about something important. Adam then went through a door leading to another room, or so I thought. I followed, and he was gone… vanished...leaving me there, with the little boy to take care of. I recall feeling supremely disappointed that my visit with Adam was cut short, but realized what was most important: taken care of the little child whom he had told that I would take care of him. I can only tell you that of all the countless dreams I have had about Adam, this dream was different from all the rest. I just can't shake the complicated feelings it evoked. I was on the verge of tears all day. However, I recall reminding myself that I now had my *"marching orders"* from him, and needed to get to work.

Backtracking a few years: When Adam was four, he began to spend his summers with me in Florida. At that time, Children's Rights of America, Inc. was headquartered in Largo, a neighboring community. I was living in a little beach efficiency apartment in Redington Shores, FL. Adam and I would usually spend our evenings walking the beach, watching the cranes and seagulls, picking up seashells, and basking in the beautiful warmth of our special relationship.

During the day, Adam would often stay with me in the offices of *Children's Rights of America,* Inc. as he would explain, *"helping my Dad."* One of the programs our agency offered was the *National Youth Crisis Hotline* (1-800-442-HOPE…which has been defunct since the organization closed its doors several years ago). We took inbound calls from children, youth, and young adults 24-hours a day, seven days a week, 365 days a year. In addition to our full-time staff, we were assisted by trained and certified volunteers. Over the years that the Hotline was operating, we took over 100,000 calls. Many callers were young people calling about everything from home problems, addiction, relationship breakups, and lack of self-acceptance. Many were *"frequent fliers"* who called us on a regular basis. However, about 1000 calls per year were *"in-progress suicide"* calls, in which callers were making a choice: live or die.

To my knowledge, we never lost a caller to suicide. Countless lives were saved. In over a decade, we averaged one *"suicide-in-progress"* call every shift, around the clock. Many of those calls were witnessed by Adam. When he was there, Adam would sometimes ask questions, and would commit to praying for the young person on the other end of the line. In fact, I often slipped him a note on a post-it, saying *"PRAY!"* Needless to say, this was a powerful experience for him; he learned a lot, and, over time, became impressed with the effectiveness of the Hotline. I became even more impressed with him. Not only was he a good listener and a good friend to so many, he practiced what he had learned about *"peeling the onion,"* making him the *"go-to"* guy for many of his friends who were struggling with issues and problems.

Starting in Middle School, Adam would often find friends who were having problems, and, rather than trying to *"fix them"* himself, he would refer them to the Hotline, sometimes dialing the number for them, and then would provide silent support as they talked to either me, or one of our Counselors. Assurance of anonymity was a vital part of our approach, so it was not uncommon for Adam to simply hand them the phone, either remaining with them, or stepping out to give them some privacy. Sometimes they said they were referred by Adam; sometimes not. What impressed me the most was that Adam had a keen sense of professionalism as a *"Referral Source."* Because of his sense of mercy, compassion, and acceptance, he was an excellent friend to have.

Often, though, Adam would call me, and would say, *"Dad, I've got this friend..."* He would then give me a brief synopsis of why he was making a referral, and put them on the line, or ask me to be expecting a call. I can't begin to describe how good it made me feel that Adam would entrust his friends to my care. I was both humbled and proud to have Adam tell me that he had told a friend, *"If my Dad can't help you, no one can. Trust me. He will find a way to help you."* Also, I never ceased to be amazed at his serious devotion to helping others ease their pain and suffering, in spite of the fact that he was dealing with so many painful issues himself. In spite of his own pain and suffering, though, ADAM NEVER FORGOT TO CARE FOR OTHERS! He realized that *"caring"* and *"loving"* were far more than mere feelings. They were Commandments given to us by our Father God.

Chapter Ten

'Genius' Is Not a Benign Condition

We were excited and proud, but not surprised, when Adam was placed in a *"Gifted and Talented"* program in Middle School. After all, he was reading like a 3rd grader when he was in the 1st grade, devouring books that I avoided when I was in High School. He was, indeed, an *"adult learner,"* trapped in a *"child learner's"* body. That particular condition led to more than a few speed bumps in Adam's road toward knowledge and enlightenment, however.

When other kids his age were focusing on rote memory and learning their multiplication tables, Adam would find himself sitting in the classroom, with eyes on greener pastures, sometimes bored to tears. He already knew how to do that stuff. Early on, though, I warned him about boredom: *"Son, boredom is a choice. It is the unfortunate end-result of a conscious and willful decision to NOT utilize the Creativity God gave you!"* After hearing that a few times, Adam learned to either choose to NOT be bored, or at least to never admit that he was bored, and to seek topics of fascination wherever he could find them.

While most of Adam's teachers in the *"Gifted and Talented"* program were to be applauded, there was one exception: his *"Creative Writing"* teacher, whom I will call *"Mr. Dimbulb"* (the name has been changed to protect the stupid). In his *"Creative Writing"* class, Adam received an assignment to write a short story. He was handed an outline on how to organize, outline, and write a short essay. Adam, as you might have guessed, had a better idea.

Instead of writing a traditional short story, Adam told his story in the form of a cartoon strip that he drew and narrated. He sent it to me before submitting it to his teacher. I thought it was brilliant and evocative. In fact, it was hilarious! I loved it! So did his Mom and Stepdad, Don. But, don't forget, I'm the Dad with a Master's Degree in Education who often offered words of wisdom to my Son such as, *"Don't forget, Son, never let your studies interfere with your high school education!"* and, *"Don't eat apples. You never know what day you're going to need a Doctor!"*

We all loved Adam's cartoon strip; everyone except his teacher, that is. I thought the strip was destined to end up in the Daily Oklahoman, if not the New York Times. I had visions of sitting on a beach, drinking umbrella drinks, while basking in the good life, as my Son --the Celebrated Cartoonist-- supported me in a manner to which I hoped to become accustomed. Unfortunately, the balloon that held my day dream aloft rapidly deflated when I learned of Adam's teacher's response to the work of the world's next Gary Larson.

Mr. Dimbulb was, shall we say, not impressed by Adam's departure from the narrow parameters of his homework assignment. You see, because Adam didn't use the cookie-cutter structural formula for a short story that his teacher had provided, he received a failing grade on the assignment. He was crestfallen, disappointed, and understandably frustrated. Me? I was livid!

"It's a CREATIVE WRITING course, for crying out loud!" I said to Deb on the phone. *"That idiot of a teacher probably flunked his first urine test, after staying up all night*

studying for it!" Debbie asked me what I thought should be done. I recommended she and Don march straight down to the school principal's office, adorned with the burning glow of the fury of a Mother and Stepfather scorned, demand that Adam's grade be revisited, and that Adam be immediately moved from that teacher's class to another one, where the teacher had a clue what *"creativity"* was. Talk about stunting creativity! I concluded my remarks by saying, *"That teacher is dumber than a bag of hair!"*

A few years later, as Adam's mental illness progressed, he suffered from chronic anxiety, depression…and a severe cognitive disorder. His psychiatric problems were exacerbated by his newfound second-favorite extra-curricular activity: getting high. Naturally, his grades slipped, but he continued to perform adequately in some of his courses, while excelling in the courses that he found most interesting. He eventually was prescribed three psychotropic medications that, unfortunately, did not mix well at all with alcohol or marijuana, and that had some uncomfortable side effects. Tragically, his self-medication to combat unpleasant his symptoms, as well as side effects of his prescribed medication, eventually led to his death.

Adam and His Dad on   **Adam and Best Friend, Bryan,**
H.S. Graduation Night   **who was with him when he died**

The Night I Met *"Leroy"*

When Adam graduated from Edmond North High School, it was a proud and exciting day for all of us. I distinctly remember several things about that ceremony and the events that followed: First of all, out of the several hundred young people who graduated that night, Adam was the only one who hugged his Principal as he walked across the stage to receive his diploma. Adam had the enlightening experience of being called into the Principal's office on quite a few occasions, largely due to the antics of Adam and his closest friends: A cohort of creative-types who remained close for years to come. I was told that he had quite a few great conversations with his Principal, who took quite a liking to him.

I was living in Clearwater, Florida, and had driven to Oklahoma to attend the festivities. Due to work demands, my time in Oklahoma was short, and I wanted to take advantage of every opportunity I could to spend time with Adam...especially since I was competing with other close family members (aunts, uncles, cousins, and grandparents), who had travelled from out of state, as well.

Following the graduation ceremony, Adam told me that he had plans to go to a movie with four of his closest friends, and that he wanted me to come along. I told him that I would not want to cramp his style, and asked if any other parents were coming. Adam said that ALL his friends thought that I was *"cool,"* and wanted me to come along...but that no other parents would be attending. I felt honored, and agreed to go.

So, we headed out to the AMC Theater in Quail Springs Mall. As we entered the Mall, and walked through the Food Court, Adam confided in me about several of his gang's most celebrated antics and public scenes that they had inflicted upon the mall visitors in the past. One, in particular, he demonstrated to me, by running through the Food Court, wildly waving his hands in the air, and screaming loudly and frantically, *"Aeyaaaaaa!"*, followed by a warning to the crowd: *"They're coming!!! Hide! Run for your lives!!!!!"* He told me that the group had about a dozen different things that they would routinely do to perplex, shock, and surprise mall visitors. They were all funny, but none could compare to what followed, after we entered the theater.

When we got inside, the theater was practically full. His four friends were able to find seats fairly close together, on the opposite side of the theater. Adam and I were fortunate enough to find two seats together, on the other side. After we sat down, Adam said, *"Now, Dad, I need to warn you. Here in a minute,*

I'm going to do something. It will be very loud, will probably embarrass you, but I promise it's hilarious." Wanting to be *"cool,"* and a *"good sport,"* I sat there, bracing myself, awaiting the antic.

The brief advertisement that asked patrons to silence their cell phones and to not talk during the movie was illustrated by an animated piece of movie film with arms and legs, taking the form of an orchestra conductor, holding a baton. Just before the Maistro raised his baton and tapped on the music stand, Adam's friends all screamed, *"Look out! The notes are gonna fall!"* As the notes fell off the piece of sheet music and plummeted to the floor, the crowd snickered and giggled; a few laughed. Then, when the crowd again became silent, Adam introduced them to his alter-ego, *"Leroy."* He began to slowly laugh in a deep, *"Suhthan,"* baritone voice, with a boisterous *"HEAH, HEAH, HEAH...HEAH, HEAH, HEAH, HEAH, HEAH, HEAH"* then loudly exclaimed, *"OH, MAH KIDNEY! OH, MAH KIDNEY! DAMN!!!"* The crowd erupted into loud laughter. I laughed so hard that my diaphragm locked up for a few moments. I couldn't breathe! It was hilarious!

Years later, as I delivered his *Eulogy*, (which is found in the Appendices of this book), I began by sharing some key words that best described Adam. When I said, *"Leroy,"* every one of the pallbearers burst out, laughing. They *"got it,"* but, of course, no one else did. That's okay. As in all of Adam's other *"Mental Hot Feet,"* the main priority was on the entertainment of him and his friends, not the puzzled crowd upon whom the jokes were inflicted.

Adam "Partying" with Friends

Chapter Eleven

Adam's Troubles, Struggles, and Suffering

During adolescence and young adulthood, Adam started experiencing some profound psychological problems, for which Debbie sought clinical help. Adam's psychiatric diagnoses varied, and, to this day, are a topic for debate among diagnosticians formerly involved in his care. At the time of his death, he was under the care of a psychiatrist, Janita M. Ardis, MD, and a clinical psychologist, John McBee, PhD. Adam's symptoms (things he felt, saw, tasted, smelled, and heard) and signs (things other people could observe, such as behaviors) varied, and were possibly caused, or exacerbated, by his abuse of alcohol and/or cannabis.

There was discussion about whether or not he suffered from schizotypal disorder or schizoaffective disorder. In addition to his mood disorders typically described as *"anxiety"* and *"clinical depression,"* he also exhibited some thought-disorder symptoms which suggested some things were going on in the schizophrenia-neck of the woods. To the casual observer, and even many of his friends and family members, however, his

107

problems went unnoticed.

Some of the hallucinations that helped lead to those diagnoses may also have been attributed to the period of time in adolescence and early adulthood when he was using cannabis on a daily basis. Until reaching their mid-20's, adolescent and young adult brains are still developing, and are sometimes more susceptible to complications due to chronic cannabis abuse. Adam was at times pretty cryptic about when and where he began to experience thought-disorder symptoms, such as hallucinations and delusions. He also minimized the extent to which he abused cannabis.

When he lived with me, he did not have much opportunity to smoke pot. There were a few times when he became intoxicated on alcohol. It was evident that, when he was drinking alcohol to the point of intoxication, he would become insulting, sarcastic, impulsive, and sometimes argumentative. In contrast, marijuana *"mellowed him out,"* Debbie told me. While I was certainly concerned with him drinking alcohol, I was particularly concerned about his marijuana abuse, because of my research on the effects on the developing adolescent brain, as well as the obvious legal issues.

Over time, his marijuana and alcohol abuse had become less frequent. After significant periods of abstinence, he was subject to occasional brief relapses, however...as he did on the night before his death. Adam had been awake for 26 hours the morning he died, was under a significant amount of stress, and had been consuming alcohol. Upon autopsy, his cardiac blood-alcohol level was found to be 0.10 % BAC; his vitreous level was 0.12 %

BAC. The legal threshold for intoxication is 0.08 %.

Although his abuse of mood/mind-altering substances had lessened as he became more focused on his ministry to the homeless, and in allowing God to use his music to *"make the world a better place, one Song at a time,"* he was legally drunk the morning he died, and, no doubt, physically exhausted…leading to his death.

Busker Statuette Placed on Adam's Tombstone

Chapter Twelve

How *"Busking University"* Was Born

In addition to his involvement in the Homeless Outreach at *The Edge Church*, Adam had a lifelong concern for those less fortunate that he was. From early childhood, he had a heart for the homeless. While he was staying with me in Atlanta, when he was eight years old, I frequently took him to a hamburger joint near downtown Atlanta, called *"The Varsity."* One afternoon, as we sat in the drive-in area of the restaurant, we watched an obviously-destitute, middle-aged man walking up to cars, begging for money to buy something to eat. There were some picnic tables near us, in an outside eating area. It appeared that the person was down on his luck, probably homeless, but he did not appear to be intoxicated. We were close enough to hear him talking. The man appeared to be coherent and sober.

When Adam asked if we could give the man some money, I said to him, *"Son, we could, but I might have a better idea. You see, that man can probably tell us the last time he ate. It might have been today, yesterday, or the day before. But, I'm willing to bet he can't tell you the last time that someone showed him some dignity and respect, and asked for his advice."* I then asked him, *"What do you think about...rather than giving him money...we order extra food and asking him to join us for lunch?"* Adam thought that was a great idea. So, as we placed our order, I ordered extra.

When our food was delivered to us by a carhop, we exited our vehicle, approached the man, and told him: *"Sir, could you do help us? We are not familiar with the Downtown Atlanta, and would like to ask you a few questions. And, we ordered more food than what we can eat. We'd like to invite you to join us for lunch, and maybe you can help us learn about the downtown area."* At that time, we were *"floor camping"* in an empty office in the corporate office suite leased by Children's Rights of America...in Cobb County, about 15 miles from the downtown area.

The man eagerly agreed to join us. I asked him if coffee was okay, or if he would prefer a soft drink. He said that he loved coffee. As we sat there, getting to know him, we asked him about the general geography, and asked him where he lived. He told us he was *"on the streets,"* having lost his apartment after he lost his job. He told us that many nights he was lucky enough to get into an area homeless shelter, but that sometimes they were full, and that he ended up sleeping wherever he could find shelter. I asked him how he stayed warm. He told us how he stuffed his clothing with newspaper, and where all a person stuck outside could find a warm, dry, and safe place to sleep.

He said that, more often than not, when he couldn't get a bed in the shelter, he slept during the day in a concealed place, when he could, because it was warmer and safer, if he remained alert and mobile at night. He said that he spent some nights riding back and forth on the MARTA train, where he was safe, as long as he remained awake. He said he could also nap sitting up, but that the rule was that passengers had to keep at least one foot on the floor at all times. He said that one travel token kept him warm all night, as he rode from one end of the train line to the other, back and forth. If the train he was on terminated at one end or the other, he would simply exit the train, wait for the next train travelling in the opposite direction, and start all over. I complimented his survival skills and strategies, which were really-well thought out. Adam was impressed with our new friend. We asked him other questions, as we all enjoyed our meal.

When we finished, I gave him ten dollars to get him another meal later, and an additional ten dollars for him to buy food to share with someone else who was hungry. The man agreed, saying that he had a friend who could use the help. I have absolutely no doubt in my mind that the man was faithful to *"pay it forward"* to a fellow homeless person. Adam was particularly taken by how the man warmed up to us, and how pleased he was that someone would ask him for help, and also trust him to share with someone else. As we parted, we told the man that we would be praying for him. I'm sure there was no doubt in the man's mind that Adam would be faithful to pray for him. There was certainly no doubt in mine.

Years later, this tradition of sharing a meal with a new friend became an important part of Adam's ministry, which was a simple-yet-powerful approach to helping the homeless. As Adam played his guitar on the streets of Oklahoma City (in *"Brick*

Town") and New York City, he would play, and people would drop money into his guitar case. He posted a little sign in the lid of the guitar case stating, *"Thanks for stopping to listen."*

When he finished playing, he would take the money he had earned, and would buy some food, finding someone less fortunate that he was to share it with. On one occasion, Adam called me, all excited, because a homeless man had put some money in the guitar case, and that somehow Adam knew to accept it. He had remembered the homeless man he had met at *The Varsity*, and how he had learned that everyone had a need to give to someone less fortunate than they were.

One day in 2004, as Adam and I were busking in a subway station in New York City, I shared with him that *"Busking is the ultimate entrepreneurship. You play to a live audience, and they have an opportunity to tip you. You don't ask for donations; just display a sign stating, 'Thanks for stopping to listen. If you earn enough money to eat, you eat. If you don't, you don't eat. It's like being a circus performer ...flying without a net."*

After Adam's death, I developed a training program for fledgling buskers, in which they could learn how to be safe, ethical, and successful street performers, and how to use their talent to convey an important message, or to *"do good for others."* The slogan for the program is, *"Training Young People to Change the World, One Song at a Time."* One week prior to the unannounced arrival of the *"Busking University Faculty,"* a one-question survey questionnaire is passed out in classes throughout a high school. Here's how it works:

The students are asked, *"If you were given $10,000, and*

could only give it to a local program in your community, would you choose (examples) A. The Battered Women's Shelter. B. The Local Juvenile Shelter. C. Food Pantry, et cetera." The survey results are tabulated, and the Recipient Program is chosen...voted for by the students. Then, the following week, a team of veteran buskers (referred to as *"Busking University Faculty"*) visit the high school, arriving the following Wednesday morning for a school assembly.

In the assembly, the *"Busking University Faculty"* talk about their life experiences as *"Street Performers,"* entertain the students, and talk about how they have used their talents to make the world a better place. They then announce a series of activities occurring during classes on Wednesday through Friday: guest speakers go to various classrooms for English Literature, English Composition, Drama, Vocal Music, Band, Art, Pottery, and Speech courses. They share their real-life busking experiences, talking more about how they use their talent to help others.

They then announce a *Busking University Talent Show,* that will be held on the following Saturday...and that there will be an opportunity for the attendees to donate financially, and that the donations will be given to the program the Student Body voted for the week prior. All students are invited to participate, either as a performer, an usher, technician, et cetera, as well as canvassing homes and businesses in town to announce the event, pass out free tickets, put up posters, et cetera. The *Busking University Young Talent Clinic* is held during the day on the Saturday following the school visit, with a dress rehearsal and Talent Show being held one week later, on the following Saturday evening.

On the night of the *Busking University Talent Show*, upon entering the auditorium, each guest is handed a program brochure, and an envelope with *"What It's Worth"* printed on the outside. Inside the envelope are coupons for freebies from local businesses, et cetera, as well as a blank credit card receipt. At the introduction of the talent show, the principal introduces the *Busking University* faculty, who in turn describe what they have been doing for the last few days.

The audience is then told that the Students had elected to donate the night's proceeds to whichever local program had gotten the most votes. The audience is invited to make a donation, based upon what the evening's performance, and the local program, was worth to them. Cash, check, and credit card donations are accepted. 100% of the proceeds go to the local benevolent charity or social program.

Additional plans for *Busking University* programs involve the top three winners being invited to perform at a *Busking University Regional Talent Show*, with the winners of those shows being sponsored to travel to a major *"busking-friendly"* city (such as New York City) for a three-day, chaperoned busking excursion. By the way, the *Busking University* program, like all other programs of the *National Crisis Intervention Training Institute*, is dedicated to the memory of Adam, who was courageous enough to *"Fly without a Net."*

Adam's Acoustic Guitar

Flying without a Net
Dedicated to Adam Joshua Johnson, Veteran Busker /
Humanitarian / Beloved Child of God

He went to cities near and far

To sing, and play his sweet guitar.

He met the eyes of passersby;

Sometimes they'd smile, sometimes they'd cry,

As sweet sounds filled the very air,

Inspiring folks to smile and share

The moment as a blessed time;

To dwell in his poetic rhyme.

He asked for nothing but an ear.

He hoped that they would truly hear

His Inner Song; that it would start

To heal a hurting, lonely heart.

As they did listen, hearts were joined.

They often shared their pocket coins,

Or dollar bills, or subway cards.
They found that sharing was not hard

To do, and that was what the lad
Had hoped they'd learn; it made him glad
For lessons learned through money shared.
He knew the needy would be spared

Another day without a meal.
He prayed his Songs would also heal
The deepest, darkest void of all:
The loneliness that oft did call

Those helpless, hurting folks to lie
In misery, in hope to die.
For he gave them more than some food;
He gave them faith in what is good:

Not just in others, but within.
Their dignity would oft begin
To be restored, as they were touched
By that Dear Lad who gave so much.

His job was simple: to reach out,
To help, to heal, and do without
So, he could take the coins he earned,
And share them with folks often spurned

And cast aside, so oft not seen
By folks who were so often mean
And cruel, and who ignored the pain;
Of those oft deemed, *"Society's Stain."*

He also gave them gifts of time
And friendship, then he'd share a rhyme,
Or song, or joke, with his new friends
To foster Dignity again.

He treated them no differently
Than other folks whose lives were free
From hunger, fear, and homelessness.
Through his kind Gift, God's Love did bless.

He'd play and sing to bring a smile
To folks who sat and waited while
Their trains approached, but didn't know
That this was no mere Music Show.

It, rather, was a Tool of Grace
To make the world a better place.
As that Sweet Minstrel ventured out
To comfort, heal, and dampen doubt

About the beauty of the soul,
He found it also made *him* whole.

He told forgotten, Homeless Ones
That they were God's Adopted Sons.

Sometimes the Homeless, sitting near
Forgot their loss, and their dark fear,
And tossed what meager coins *they* had
Into the hat of that Sweet Lad.

In wisdom he did not refuse;
He saw their need to give and choose
To act in new-found dignity;
Their *"Widow's Mite"* made their hearts free.

He long ago gave God his gift,
Although his pain inside did sift
And tear apart his Inner Peace;
But he did not let his heart cease

To beat with love, until he lost
His earthly life, when it was tossed
Aside on a most tragic day,
When bullets took his life away.

But rest assured he did not fear
To seek folks out, and draw them near.
Now he lives on in Hearts of Men
Who've learned to love themselves again.

Because of simple acts of love
Through that Dear Lad, from God Above,
His Music rings inside their souls
As they rejoice, now that they're whole,

Because a Friend flew far above,
Without a Net, to share God's Love.
He shared his life, his Song, his meal,
So God could Touch, Restore, and Heal.

Copyright 2011, Joel Johnson

Chapter Thirteen

Busking and Delivering Mental Hot Feet in the Big Apple

Adam Playing Guitar on Our *"Stoop"* in Brooklyn, NY

I lived in Brooklyn, NY twice…for two years each time: 1999-2001, and 2003-2005. Of those four years, 2004 was, by far, the most fun. Adam came to live with me that year…and, man, did we have a blast! The two of us lived in a quaint little basement apartment in Bay Ridge…one of the nicest neighborhoods in Brooklyn. I rented the apartment from a dear friend, Ramesh Kristi, who worked with me in the Emergency Room of *Maimonides Medical Center.*

Adam and I had many types of adventures: furniture shopping in Manhattan…between midnight and 5:00am (looking for discarded throwaways…primo stuff, by the way)…venturing into Manhattan at 3:00am for hotdogs and smoothies at *Gray's Papaya*, and busking in our favorite haunts: *Port Authority, Grand Central Station, Penn Station, 34th Street Station,*

Washington Square Park, and *Central Park.* We even played *AT Carnegie Hall*…we just never actually made it *INTO* Carnegie Hall. But we could honestly say, *"We played AT Carnegie Hall."* We got about ten feet from the front door. We put a sign on Adam's guitar case lid that said: *"Working our way inside!"*

Adam took to busking, New York-Style, like a fish to water. His favorite gig, however, was the honor of playing on the stoop of our basement apartment in Bay Ridge, Brooklyn. Why? Because we lived right next door to Liberty DeVitto, who was Billy Joel's drummer for thirty years. On one occasion I remember in particular, *"Lib"* came out onto the stoop with some bongos, and jammed with Adam. I didn't play that day…I just sat and watched the look of joy on my Son's face…playing with one of his all-time musical heroes, and quite possibly the world's best living drummer. Adam loved Liberty, and Liberty loved him. About three mornings a week, Adam and I would go over to Lib's house for bagels and coffee. We called it, *"Brunch at Liberty's."* At Christmas time, we met his daughter, Torrey DeVitto, who now has a starring role on the television show, *"Chicago Med."*

Of all our NYC musical adventures, there are three busking excursions that really stand out in my library of memories: In the first one, Adam and I were riding the *"R"* train back to Brooklyn, on a near-full subway car. Adam took out his guitar, announced to the crowd that they should relax and hang on to their money, that we were not accepting any tips or donations. The main reason we weren't accepting money is that it was a slight fracture of the city ordinances to solicit donations in the subway cars…primarily because people riding the train were a captive

124

audience. The second reason was that Adam and I were primarily motivated by the desire to instill a little comradery and togetherness among our fellow passengers.

As Adam started to strum out an *"Intro,"* I walked the length of the subway car, inviting the crowd to snap along with me in time to the music. Pretty soon, the whole car...young, old, rich, poor, *EVERY* body was snapping their fingers! Then Adam quit playing for a moment, and the passengers kept on snapping; no doubt wondering what was coming next. I announced to the people that we were going to engage in a little experiment: that at the next stop, people getting off the train should keep snapping their fingers, as did the passengers remaining in the subway car.

People entering the train were perplexed at our behavior, because, from our appearances, it was pretty obvious that the people were strangers from all walks of life. As people entered the car and found a place to sit or stand, I coached them to join in. Then, once the car was rolling again, Adam started playing once more. It was what we called, *"A New York Moment."*

The second incident happened one day, when Adam and I got to the Port Authority a bit late, finding that all three of our usual spots to stand were taken. So, we resorted to going down onto the loading and unloading platform of a really busy train that had arrivals and departures every two to three minutes. It was LOUD! Adam became a bit frustrated because he could not get through an entire Song in without being interrupted by the loud noise of the train...so, he improvised. There was a dividing platform between two opposite-running tracks.

Adam started in with an improvisation that we later

called, *"Hey, People on That Side."* The lyrics were *"Hey, people on that side...our side's cooler than yours."* He would repeat that refrain, then say, *"All you got is a guy with blue pants...and we got a lady with a beautiful hat,"* etc. etc. He was pointing out the apparel or physical characteristics of people in the crowd. Pretty soon we had people clapping along with the Song, and laughing at the improvised lyrics. One or two even took a bow when their outstanding physical characteristic was mentioned in the Song. Not only did it lift Adam's mood, it resulted in great tips!

The third busking highlight occurred during the *Republican National Convention*, held at *Madison Square Garden* from August 30, 2004 to September 2, 2004. During that event, many disgruntled Democrats were engaging in some pretty disruptive protesting outbursts. NYPD had encased a large parking lot in Manhattan with chain-link fencing, and started arresting disruptive protesters for Disorderly Conduct (which was a "violation," not a misdemeanor), confining them in the fenced-in area, until particular events were over, at which time they simply issued a Desk Appearance Ticket to the detainees. It was a 14-karat mess in Manhattan for those four days.

On one particular day of the Convention, the Vice President was in town. We got to *Port Authority*, as usual, I muttered, *"Houston, we have a problem."* There was not a busker in sight. As we entered a wide-open area where we usually played, we observed three members of *New York's Finest* standing together: two Patrol Officers and a Sergeant. I approached and said, *"Hey, guys. As a trained observer, it would appear that there is no busking allowed today."* One officer said, *"Yes, Sir.*

We'll have to ask you to move along. [Vice President] Cheney is coming through in a little bit, and the bosses ordered us to keep everyone moving," at which point the Sergeant told his officers, *"Let these guys play for a little while. I heard them last week, and they're good!"*

We played a couple of their requests, and then a couple of our regular tunes. After about 15 minutes, the Sergeant got a call on his handheld radio, and said, *"He's coming through. Guys, sorry. The Lieutenant just told me the mess is about to begin. You'll need to move along. Thanks for playing, though. Catch you next time!"* The Sergeant then walked over and dropped a ten-dollar bill into Adam's guitar case. We spent it on pizza.

We resided in Brooklyn, but we *LIVED* in Manhattan. For the four years I was there, I spent every available living moment in the *"City that Never Sleeps."* I loved walking around the city, riding the subway, driving in the wee hours of the night, and exploring new places. As an incorrigible *"people watcher,"* I loved watching the *"million stories [in that] naked city."* I was not bored for a single moment, during my tenure as a "New Yorker."

Most of all, I loved introducing Adam to the *"Big Apple."* Aside from our Number One love (busking), we enjoyed people watching, and giving people what George Carlin referred to as *"Mental Hot Feet"* (which meant doing something in front of, or to, a total stranger that would assure that you would be *"renting free space"* in that person's head for the rest of the day). We did so many during that year, but one of my favorites was a joke we pulled in the *Michelangelo Hotel*, located at 152 W. 51st Street.

One day, during the summer, Adam and I were walking around Midtown Manhattan, on one of our non-busking adventure days. We had spent some time in Times Square, walked uptown a few blocks, then turned right onto 51st Street, on our way to *Radio City Music Hall* and *Rockefeller Center*. We hadn't done a *"Mental Hot Foot"* that day. As we walked by the entrance to the *Michelangelo Hotel*, I was *"stricken by the Mental Hot Foot Muse,"* meaning that I had a sudden idea for a prank. I said to Adam, *"Son, follow my lead on this one. I have an idea."*

We walked into the majestic lobby, looked around, and spotted a beautiful, tall, and statuesque young woman standing behind the front desk. I walked up to her, with Adam following, and was greeted by a bright smile, and an inquiring, *"Good afternoon, how may I help you?"* I responded, *"Yes, Miss...my name is John Sistine. My family owns the Sistine Chapel in Rome, Italy. My associate and I have come to New York to paint the ceiling of your hotel lobby."* I could hear Adam snort through his nose behind me. The young woman said, *"Excuse me?"* I repeated, *"You have certainly heard of the Sistine Chapel."*

I could tell by her hesitant response that she probably had not. So, I went on to say, *"Well, allow me to explain. You all did such a remarkable job of painting the ceiling of our chapel a few years ago; so my father, James Sistine, sent us over here to paint the ceiling of your hotel lobby. This IS the only Michelangelo*

Hotel in New York, correct?" She replied, "Uh, yes, I believe so."
I felt that, at this point, she surely would have gotten the joke, but she evidently had not: She pulled out a three-ring binder and started looking through it for a work order!

After leafing through several pages, she said, "Sir, I don't show any record of a work order for you to be here." I said, "That's impossible. There must be some mistake. We would not have travelled several thousand miles without the project being confirmed. Please tell me, is the Day Manager on duty, or the Night Manager?" The young woman replied, "The Day Manager is on duty; he is out at the moment. He will be returning shortly." I said, "Well, that explains it. Due to the time difference. We always spoke to the Night Manager."

I then asked for a piece of paper, grabbed an ink pen from the counter, and wrote down the following bullet points: "John Sistine, Family Owns Sistine Chapel. Here to paint ceiling of the Michelangelo Hotel lobby." Handing it to her, I said, "Please ask the Day Manager to Call the Night Manager to confirm the work order. We have the rental van parked just down the block with the paint, tarps, and scaffolding. It should be okay for a little while. We are going to go grab a bite; will be back in about hour."

I found it both interesting and hilarious that, after telling her that I was from Rome, Italy, that my "Okie" accent was never questioned. Adam and I then exited the hotel, and, upon reaching the sidewalk, burst out in laughter. Adam said, "That was excellent." He then got a bit of concerned look on his face, and then said, "Dad, you realize she will probably get fired for being so dumb, right?" I said, "Son, I somehow suspect it was not her *intellect that got her hired to begin with. I'm sure her job is safe."*

Another day, we were driving in Brooklyn, and spied a business with a sign saying, *"Self-Storage."* I pulled in to the parking area, walked in the front door of the business with Adam, and perused through a list of storage unit prices on the wall. The units started at $295 per month. I then approached the man behind the counter, and said, *"Hi. I am interested in storing myself in one of your units, but I have just a few questions first."* The man replied, *"Huh?"* So, I repeated, *"Well your sign says, 'Self-Storage. I am interested in storing myself here. Your rates are excellent; far cheaper than my current apartment rent. But I noticed that your sign outside also said that no one is allowed into the building after 8pm. That's just fine, but I work the night shift, from 11pm to 7am. So, I need to know, am I allowed to LEAVE after 8pm? That's important, because if I am stuck here all night, and can't get to work, I'll lose my job."*

The man looked at me like I was some kind of nut, and said, *"Are you a @#+)#@) idiot?"* I replied, *"You know, you're the third person to ask me that today; I assure you I am not."* I looked at Adam, who nodded his head, and said, *"He's not."* The man then stated, with a thick Brooklyn accent, *"You store your #%*$ here!"* I then stated, *"Oh, my! I would think the smell would be terrible! I figured I'd go in a bucket with a bag in it, then carry the bag out when I went to work."* It was at this point that Adam burst out laughing, and the man cordially invited us to exit his business post-haste. That was a perfect example of how and why I developed the exit line, *"Sir, I'll have you know that I've been kicked out of MUCH nicer places than this!"*

Chapter Fourteen

Adam at the Academy of Recording Arts

Fourteen months prior to his death, Adam graduated from the *Academy of Recording Arts*, in Oklahoma City, OK, receiving his *Diploma of Audio Recording Engineering*. I had the great honor of being asked by Adam to travel to Oklahoma City, along with my esteemed guitarist, Teresa Arruza, to record 36 Songs (filling three CDs) as his Final Project toward completion of his program. Teresa and I were, at the time, playing together in *"The Moon Glow Duo."* We busked on the streets and beaches of St. Petersburg, FL, as well as a variety of venues such as wineries, fine restaurants, hotels, and outdoor music festivals.

When we flew to Oklahoma City, Teresa did not have a hard-sided guitar case, so she travelled without her guitar, and used Adam's acoustic guitar to record our three CDs, entitled, *"Moonglow,"* *"Summertime,"* and *"It's Beginning to Look a Lot Like Christmas."* We spent only three afternoons in the studio. Adam did a masterful job of sound mixing, recording, followed up by some incredible sound engineering. He later told me that his instructor informed him that we had set an all-time record for the number of Songs recorded in a three-day period, with the exception of one other musician who was recorded as a guitar soloist.

After Adam's death, I had another engineer compose a CD of nineteen of the most popular Songs from our three CDs, adding the only recording we ever did of *"The Notes of Adam's Song,"* which I wrote the night before Adam's funeral, and recorded several months later. As I listen to our music today, I am particularly blessed, because the guitar Teresa was playing was Adam's guitar.

Adam did not have the opportunity to pursue a professional career as a sound engineer, but we all view his accomplishment as a major highlight of his young life. Thanks to Adam, who chose me to be a part of his Final Project, he lives on in my musical legacy.

Chapter Fifteen

I Liked the Way He Talked

Of all the movies that we both loved, Adam and I regarded *"Sling Blade"* as being at the top of our list. Two pieces of movie dialog stood out as favorites were when Karl and his new, young friend Frank engaged in a bit of mutual admiration: Frank said, *"I like the way you talk,"* and Karl responded with, *"I like the way YOU talk."* We repeated that exchange to each other hundreds of times.

Another favorite piece of dialog from the movie was when Doyle, the cruel, drunken stepfather of Frank, was speaking ill of his stepson, and Karl responded, in defense of Frank*, "Don't you go saying nuthin' bad about that boy!"* Many times, when Adam was putting himself down, or being overly-self-critical, I would respond in Karl's voice, telling him, *"Don't you go saying nuthin' bad about that boy!"* as a playful and gentle reminder for Adam to lighten up on himself, to realize how special he was…and what a blessing he was to so many people.

During my darkest moments, when the pain of separation and loss become unbearable, I often repeat that dialog out loud, remembering, and looking forward to once again holding his hand one day. Here is an old Facebook entry, describing one of those moments, posted by me the night of January 7, 2013, at 9:30 pm:

I Like the Way You Talk

(Posted on Facebook on the night of January 7, 2013)

In eight hours, it will be four years since the Lord graciously accepted my beloved Son Adam into Heaven, after his life was violently taken away. The pain and profound sense of loss and emptiness still reside in this Dad's broken heart...But so does the hope of one day being reunited with a young man who taught me far more than I could ever have hoped to teach him.

Adam believed that actions were the only form of "talking" that really mattered. As a true grass roots humanitarian who believed in letting others see his faith in Christ, Adam desired to be used by God to touch many lives, and to make the world a better, kinder, gentler, and infinitely more amusing place to live. Creating music was his passion, and he wrote some beautiful music. However, the most beautiful Song ever written by Adam was written and performed with his life's actions toward others.

The night before his funeral, I wrote a Song in his honor, called "The Notes of Adam's Song." The chorus of that Song is etched on his tombstone, as his loving memory is engraved forever on my heart.

"Son, your smile is our melody; your heart is our harmony, and the lyrics of your life, they make us strong. Our love for you will stay, and will never go away...for we are The Notes Adam's Song."

I love you, my Son...and I like the way you talk. Love, Dad

Chapter Sixteen

How Adam Lived / About Adam's Battle Cry

Approximately two years prior to his death, Adam called and left a phone message for me. I still have the message saved on my desktop computer. It said, *"Hey, Dad...I know it's late, but I've been having some pretty good thoughts lately about some things, and just wanted to share them with you. If you're still up, cool. If not, I'll talk to you tomorrow. Love ya. Bye."*

I called him back the next morning, and he emailed me his *"Battle Cry for a New Christian Initiative,"* asking me to read it, and to give him feedback and guidance. After I finished reading it, I silently thought how proud I was of his zeal and sincerity, and then said to myself, *"Oh, Boy! Is THIS gonna tick some people off!"* I started out by sharing with him that I felt he was *"right on"* about what he recognized as society's failings; that he was absolutely correct about our hypocrisy and selfishness; and that he had hit the nail on the head about how God's children had fallen short of God's Glory.

Then I offered some *"cautionary guidance,"* about how to share the information without having doors slammed in his face, rather than telling him to *"go for it."* I told him that things generally turned out badly for most of the true prophets in the Old and New Testaments, and that he should carefully and prayerfully seek out guidance from God in how to share his message with God's people. I told him it would be a good idea to make an appointment with his Pastor, Israel Hogue, to get to know him better, and to share his *"Battle Cry"* with him, which he did within a week of our phone conversation.

Two years later, after Adam's death --in Deb's living room-- Israel shared with us about the first time he met Adam, and was privileged to hear Adam deliver his *"Battle Cry"* in his office. Our conversation took place two days before Adam's funeral. Israel told me that he had two vivid memories of Adam, which he planned on sharing with the celebration of Adam's life: First, he shared about the day that Adam came into his office and told Israel that God had given him a message that he wanted to share with the church body at *The Edge Church*.

At Israel's invitation, Adam read his *"Battle Cry"* aloud, in what Israel described as Adam's --let's just call it-- animated style; how he stood in the middle of Israel's office as if he was standing before the congregation, and read the document with such passion and sincerity, sometimes with tears in his eyes. He all but nailed his treatise onto the door, Martin Luther-style.

Israel did not share everything that he said to Adam in response, other than he was extremely impressed with Adam's sense of justice, fairness, and honesty; that it was clear that he was genuinely passionate in his resolve to serve God...and that Israel was very proud and happy to have him as a member of *The Edge Church.* Adam did not end up delivering his message during a church service, however. Israel then chuckled as he shared that, after Adam left his office, his secretary entered his office, wide-eyed and grinning from ear to ear, and asked, *"What in the world was that?"* Israel responded with pride and a smile, *"That's Adam Johnson, and he goes here*

Israel then shared that his other vivid, and favorite memory of Adam was the day that, during the offertory, with

Praise Team music blaring, Adam got up, ran down the aisle, slide forward to the altar on his knees, and played *"Air Guitar"* with the band, in joyous celebration of his faith and gratitude toward God. I quipped that I had often told my Son, if he could somehow overcome his shyness, he had a real future as a public speaker.

I have re-read Adam's treatise several times over the course of the last eleven years, and each and every time I have thought more about the *"advice"* I gave him, with some regrets: I told him that perhaps he was covering a lot of material on many subjects, and that the treatise in its entirety was pretty overwhelming; that he might want to consider breaking it up into a series of confrontational messages; that it was important to present the material in a way that did not slam doors shut before they had been opened, yada, yada.

I will regret that for the rest of my life, and I'm not even sure that I should. I may have been right. Sometimes when I am lying awake in the dark at three o'clock in the morning, the fears, regrets, and doubts hit me. What I fear the most is that my *"discretion is the better part of valor,"* and *"timing is everything"* rhetoric may have discouraged Adam from confronting what he believed to be wrongs being committed by the Body of Christ, and that I may have unintentionally stifled his desire to cry out in outrage; and to challenge people who really needed to hear it, to look honestly into themselves...and repent.

Out of what I thought was a desire to protect my Son from being embarrassed, or even worse, discouraged, I sometimes fear that I perhaps had unintentionally been a source of discouragement. He may have thought through what I said, and decided that I was right...even though, in retrospect, I quite possibly wasn't. As I said, he never shared this message in its entirety with his Church Family, but after his meeting with Pastor Hogue, he enthusiastically dove right in, and became actively involved in the church's ministry to the homeless. He worshipped there regularly, and genuinely loved his church family at *The Edge Church*.

I hope that this book sells a million copies...not because of the possibility of financial gain, but because it will give a million people the opportunity to look within the core of a courageous, truly-good young man, whose grass roots humanitarianism and social conscience were born out of his desire to be obedient to God, and to be a terrific steward over the earth, its resources, and especially, God's children. Out of respect for my Son, I chose to not edit his treatise. It is printed exactly as he wrote it. He entitled it:

Battle Cry for a New Christian Initiative

"Good morning ladies and gentlemen. Before I get started, I'd like to share a bit about myself. I will keep it brief, though, because my message is too important to wait much longer. My name is Adam Johnson. I'm twenty-two years old, I work as a delivery driver at Pizza Hut on 33rd and Boulevard in Edmond, and I'm attending classes at the Academy of Recording Arts in Oklahoma City to learn how to be a studio engineer and record producer. God has called upon me to share a message with you all, and share it, I must, because I feel that it is far too important to this world to keep locked away in my mind. I wish I could say

to you that I'm bringing a message of joy, of happiness, of contentment. This is not the case.

I'm bringing you a message of suffering, sorrow, and the need for action on the part of Christians everywhere. This speech is not a call for you to rejoice in your salvation. It is a battle cry for a new type of battle, with a new way of fighting. I have asked that only people age 14 and up attend this service because I am touching on some heavier issues and I just feel it is best this way. If you have younger children or family members who couldn't make it today but you wish them to hear this message, there will be a number of ways for you to get a copy of this message, which we'll discuss after today's service. It isn't my wish to make anyone here feel bad about anything, but I'm going to make some very harsh, very REAL points, and feeling bad may just be an inevitability. I wish it could be different, but if it could be different, I probably wouldn't need to be here.

The world is falling apart. Plain and simple. Children in Uganda are being taken from their families, guns forced into their hands, being brainwashed and made into murderers, many by their 10th birthdays, to fight a war over diamonds. Diamonds they will never get to see. Shiny, rare, little stones that will give profits to a number of people, but not one cent, not one grain of rice, even, to the people who are actually fighting and dying for them. Officials in South Africa are supplying the public with bad information about HIV and AIDS, telling the people that HIV doesn't always lead to AIDS, and essentially indicating to the masses that having HIV is not a reason to stop having sex. These messages are targeted specifically at educationally and socio-

Economically-disadvantaged peoples.

The only purpose of this that I can deduce is that the people in power are hoping to get them to all infect each other and kill each other off so the ruling classes don't need to be bothered with the poor anymore. The greatest travesty in our world right now, though, is one which everyone here is closely involved in. Christian Americans, with all of their material and spiritual blessings, are doing little to nothing to change the state of the world. It fills me with rage. Initially I was angry at God, wondering why he was letting all of this horrible garbage go on, convinced that he was just really bad at his job. Then the answer was staring me in the face. God made it abundantly clear that he wasn't going to do everything for us. He made it clear to me that Christian Americans have a higher duty to the world than anyone, because we are in the best position to help change things.

Everything you think you've been doing to help the world isn't enough. If it was, the world would be in better condition. Look at the crusades! Hate-mongering and murder in the name of God! No wonder we couldn't convert the Muslims! I'm not saying that some of the crusaders weren't well-intentioned, that they didn't honestly believe that they were doing God's work. I'm just saying that there is a big difference between thinking or believing you're doing God's work and actually DOING God's work. The same thing has happened in our time. The late Reverend Falwell is a prime example. This man insisted that 9/11 was God punishing us for being lenient on and accepting of adulterers, homosexuals, feminists, and so on.

There is a fundamental flaw in his line of thinking. Christ, above all else, taught us to be compassionate and accepting of EVERYONE. Why? Because we are all sinners. Homosexuals have become a target of hate from a lot of Christians and religious Conservatives in general, and sadly these Christians are somehow blind to their own hypocrisy. Homosexuality has become some sort of ultra-sin in the eyes of many Christians, even though the bible they thump so loudly explicitly says that ALL SINS ARE EQUAL IN THE EYES OF GOD. This means that a gay man is no more or less guilty than a liar, an alcoholic, a gossip, a murderer, or a thief. All of us are sinners, and Christ's whole point was not to crush the spirit of the sinner, but to lift that person up. Not to pass judgment or speak ill of them, but to pick them up, accept them for who they are, and guide them to peace; because we are all the same.

Perhaps the Reverend Falwell truly did believe God was punishing us. Well-intentioned or not, he was definitely deluded. I pose this question to those who agree with his stance: Since when does God punish his followers for doing exactly what Christ wanted them to do? This is my battle cry. A new type of battle is in our hands. A battle that involves no guns, nor knives, nor words of hate, but one that involves a conscious choice on the part of all Christians in this country, Baptist, Methodist, Presbyterian, whatever, to stand up and live the lives Christ would want us to, and to handle the problems this world faces us with in a Christ-like way.

For too long Christians in this country have just been showing up to church, expressing their belief that Christ granted us forgiveness of our sins, and throwing some money in the

141

collection plate, then patting themselves on the back for being such good little Christians. Yes, the bible said to do all these things. It didn't say to stop there. That's why I'm here. Too many people in this country, too many people in this BUILDING, are stopping there. Too many of us have become complacent. You know what that means? I'm not giving you a dictionary definition; I'm giving you my own personal definition. Complacency means, essentially, that you think things are going alright, so why do anything else? You're getting by, so why do anything else? This is FUNDAMENTALLY UN-CHRIST-LIKE.

Christ never would have wanted us to become so self-satisfied and self-absorbed. The next time you sit down to watch the news and you see a story of tragedy and human suffering, ask yourself "What would Jesus do?" I guarantee he would do more than just say a prayer for those in need and go to bed, resolved to give an extra twenty bucks on Sunday. He would have gotten off his butt and gone out into the world to try to do something. That's why I'm here. To spark some interest in being more Christ-like.

I'm not talking about telling fewer lies or taking fewer drinks or kissing fewer girls. Those things are minor details. I'm talking about taking an initiative for the God who has done so much for us. He's given the people of this country SO MUCH, and relatively speaking we've done SO LITTLE with it.

God has given us near-unlimited resources, and many in this country have chosen to squander their wealth on bigger cars, bigger TVs, bigger houses, not because they NEED the extra cargo capacity or 23 inches of screen or 2 extra bedrooms and an extra bathroom they'll hardly ever use, but because this shameful, faulty mentality of "bigger is better" has become so synonymous with the American way of life.

It's become so engrained that even as Christians we're blind to it, we fall victim to it. I was mad at God. I was incredibly mad at Him, not for my sake, but for the sake of all the innocent people out in the world suffering while he stands by and lets it happen. Then it hit me. It was staring me in the face. God never said he was going to do everything for us. WE are the ones standing by doing nothing while the world falls apart around us. It's not up to God to help the world, it's up to us.

I'm not just here to make you feel bad about it, don't worry. I've brought some suggestions and some solutions with me today. Many of these are very simple things that everyone can take part in. It isn't God's intention for everyone here to go on a mission trip to South Africa, I don't believe it's his intention for everyone here to get up and do what I'm doing. I do believe He has a place in this new initiative for every person here, though, whether it is a lofty position filled with responsibilities and trials, or a small position of support. I am pleading with all of you to at least do SOMETHING. If everyone in here at least does one tiny thing that I suggest, the world will be a better place all around, whether you are a Christian, a Muslim, a Jew, a Buddhist, or an atheist.

One very important thing that Christ did was to lead by example. He didn't tell us the way, HE TRIED TO SHOW US THE WAY. Sadly, I fear, we missed the point in a lot of ways. The bible calls us to lead the world to Christ. As I mentioned earlier, I believe we've been going about this the wrong way for centuries.

Look at the example we're setting as Americans. We're showing the world that it's okay to rest on our laurels, to get caught up so much in materialism and vanity while so many suffer all around us. THAT'S why we've failed.

We haven't truly been practicing what we preach. Sure, most of us aren't killers or liars or thieves or what the world as a whole would label as "bad people," and in that respect we have been doing a good job. However, when the rest of the world look at all of our material wealth, watch the money we spend on absurdly large, over-powered cars, cosmetic surgery, and male enhancement pills, they see something in total contradiction to being Christ-like. I know I do. I know I see a room filled with people that have a desire for God, but because of the way the world is have lost focus on what's really important in life. I see a room full of people who need some good ideas of what to do with their wealth.

For six thousand dollars we can build an orphanage in Cambodia to house twelve children who would otherwise end up in the sex trade. The average cost of breast implant surgery starts around $3000. If twenty women decided to leave their boobs the way they are and give that money to a charity building these orphanages we could house 120 children who would otherwise become sex slaves! You all believe that God has blessed you all so much, yet you sit amongst all your blessings with a sense of self-satisfaction unbefitting someone who truly loves Christ. I'm not saying that we should feel bad about it, that doesn't accomplish anything. I'm just asking that everyone here acknowledge the truth in my words and make a decision to change *things, because that's what Christ wants, and if he were walking the earth here today that's what he would be doing.*

So now I've gotten you all riled up a little, gotten into your heads a little, attacked your ways of life a little, and now a lot of you are probably looking at me thinking "Well what makes you so bloody great, what are you doing that makes you so special, and how much money are you going to ask us for, where's the part where you ask for my credit card number?!?" I don't need your money, I'm not any more special than anyone else here, and I'm not doing anything THAT big. Not yet. Right now, I'm trying to do what I can when I can. That's the key.

I'm going to start with an example that touches the lives of everyone in this country. Let's talk about gas prices for a second. Do you know why gas prices are so high? It isn't why you think. It isn't the war. It's our own fault. Granted, the war is a contributing factor, but not the main one. Let me explain. If you've taken even a high school economics course this information is not going to be new to you, it's just going to surprise you that you've never realized it until now, and that with all of the economists at our government's disposal none of them have realized it either. It's all about supply and demand. For right now people believe that the war is the reason supply is down, which is why demand is up, which is why the price is so high. WRONG!!!!! Demand is up because so many people in this country insist on driving vehicles they just plain don't need.

I'm talking about Hummers, Expeditions, Excursions, Escalades, Navigators, Mustang GTs, Cobras, Trans-Ams, SS Camaros, and so on. What do all of these have in common? At least 80% of the people who drive them, by my estimation, don't actually have a necessity for such power in their vehicles. I consider that estimation very generous, but I'm not a statistician, so I can't make any guarantees on the math. I'll just call it an educated guess. Let's say you bought a new H3, which gets an EPA estimated 15 miles per gallon in the city. How many insurgents do you guys have to fight every day? How many days a week are you towing a trailer or a boat? How many times in a week do you even have the seats in the thing filled? The answers are probably none, none, and few to none.

I spend a lot of time on the road, driving a beat up old '89 Honda Accord to deliver pizza, and I see a lot of vehicles just like this H3 I've described with only one person inside or maybe two. This is just an unwise use of energy. I don't drive the Honda because I have to, by the way. I could be driving a much more comfortable Jeep Cherokee with a 4.0 liter inline-six, a nice CD player and a halfway decent audio system. Instead I opt to park it during my work week and trade it for something that gets better gas mileage. "So what?" you ask. "You get better gas mileage and you're saving yourself money, how is that being Christ-like, how is that helping anyone but yourself?"

Here's the big moment, are you guys ready? If everyone who had the means to begin driving more economical vehicles did so, if they parked their big SUVs and sports cars during their work week and replaced them with more sensible vehicles, the demand for gasoline would decrease dramatically. What happens when demand decreases? Supply increases! And what happens when supply increases? Say it with me people: PRICE GOES DOWN!

If we make these small changes and the price does go down, then everyone will have more money to spend on entertainment, food, clothing, whatever else, which will stimulate the economy like crazy, put a damper on all of this inflation, and bring the value of the American dollar back up to a point where it actually competes with Europe and China again, and give some much-needed relief to our middle and lower class brothers and sisters!

"So what, Adam, you mean I'm supposed to sacrifice some of my own comforts to help the rest of the country, even though a bunch of these people aren't the same as me and I don't agree with their beliefs?" YES!!! YES YES YES YES YES!!!!!!!!!! THAT'S WHAT CHRIST WANTED US TO DO. HE DIDN'T WANT US TO RUN AROUND IMPOSING OUR BELIEFS ON PEOPLE! HE WANTED US TO LIVE BY OUR BELIEFS AND LET THAT BE AN EXAMPLE TO OTHER PEOPLE, IN A HOPE OF LEADING THEM IN THE RIGHT DIRECTION!!!!

I don't just drive the Honda because it's cheaper. I could afford to drive the Jeep around just fine, just like even at three dollars per gallon the people in here who drive these unnecessary vehicles can afford it. I drive the Honda instead because I feel a sense of duty, a sense of obligation to the people in this country, to the people of the world, to do something to try to make it better!

I'm not pushing an environmentalist agenda. I know a lot of people, Christians or otherwise, who see environmentalism as some silly liberal agenda, as something unnecessary to our survival. I find it odd for Christians to feel this way since one of the very first assignments God gave to man was for him to tend to the Earth, to take care of it! It's in Genesis, people! I'm a New

Testament kind of guy, without a doubt, but I have to go back to the classics for this one! It's our duty as Christians to do something to help the planet. Think about the effect it would have on the world's view of Christians, of Americans in general, if we all took up an initiative to change the world and make it a better place, instead of just running around trying to tell people what they should believe!

Wouldn't it be nice to be able to say "I'm proud to be an American" and actually have something to be proud of! Imagine how much better this place would be if we started putting to use all of the blessings God has given us. A member of Crossings Community Church, a man I respect as a friend, a neighbor, and a Christian told me he believed there was nothing we could do to destroy this planet; that God wouldn't allow it. I disagree whole-heartedly.

From my perspective, as far as I can tell, God is more than willing to let us obliterate this place and suffer the consequences for it. There are enough nuclear weapons in place on this planet to turn it all into a giant cloud of dust. That's why it's so important for us to take this initiative. You might say, "Well, I have faith in the Lord, he'll take care of us." Not if we aren't willing to help take care of ourselves and take care of the rest of the world.

Now, we aren't perfect and we can't accomplish everything. God's own perfect Son didn't fix everything in the world, He just sparked the fire. He had to rely on the help of friends, the help of strangers, and the help of God to accomplish what He set out to do. We can't do everything, but we can at least make an effort. Bravo for all of the missionaries, all of the people reaching out to our Muslim brothers and sisters, our Jewish brothers and sisters, our homosexual brothers and sisters. Shame on the rest of us, though, for sitting idly by, too caught up in our own lives to realize that we have it so good compared to the rest of the world. I know many of you here are struggling.

Struggling to stay happy, struggling to get by, to keep faith, to figure out how you'll pay your bills. I understand this, and so does God. Take it from a man who has seen it work in his own life, someone who has first-hand experience with the power of God, the power of Christ; sew a seed of faith, something small, but something, and God will make it grow! It will only take a little, tiny bit on each person's part, and the results will be astounding!

There are many solutions to many problems, many ways to make changes in the world. The gas example was just a starter because it affects everyone in here. How many people in here have seen a homeless person in the past month? How many of you decided not to give him or her money because you decided he or she would spend it on booze or drugs?

The thought crosses everyone's mind at some point. I realized this is not the Christ-like way of doing things. It's not your place to judge them. They may or may not be wrong in the eyes of God for what they do with the money they receive, but you are twice guilty, first for passing judgment against them, and again for allowing your judgment to justify selfishness and greed. I've done it, too! I've tried to convince myself I was helping the guy by not giving him any cash.

If you truly believe in God, you must assume that God will

149

see that you've helped this person in good faith, and that He will work things out from there. That couple of dollars you give that needy person could be more to them than just a means to acquire instant gratification. It could be that this person really did just want something delicious to eat, or it could be that this act of kindness is enough to resolve them to push on for one more day, and it may be that the very next day a Christian in despair will see that same needy person and find a new sense of resolve, a breath of fresh air, a new reason to keep living as a Christian and keep working to make the world better. In this situation, your small act of kindness would have saved two lives! Christ would have given money to the homeless without passing judgment; he may have even invited them to lunch, in spite of them smelling to high heaven!

So what changes am I talking about? If you think I'm talking about converting everyone in the world to Christianity, you are sorely mistaken. This is one mistake Christians have been making since the very beginning. We've been going around TELLING people that our answer was right and everyone else's is wrong. If there's one thing I know about dealing with people, it's that NO ONE LIKES TO HEAR HOW WRONG THEY ARE. It has gotten so ridiculously out of hand, time and time again, down through the centuries, and has only proven to me that, by and large, the way Christians have been doing things is not the way Christ would have wanted it.

The next time you see something lying in the middle of the road that could be dangerous to other drivers, stop and move it! Don't assume someone else will get around to it or that everyone will be able to avoid it like you did. DO something about it. Pick up a piece of trash in your neighbor's yard. Sacrifice your Saturday night to baby sit for a friend who doesn't get to go out much. Help a stranger carry something heavy to his or her car! Tip your pizza guy! That's one of my personal favorites! The list will go on and on.

I'll be compiling a list of small things everyone can do and posting it on a myspace.com page, so if people are just having a really hard time thinking of things that would help, they'll have a place to turn to get some ideas. Also, if you have good ideas, we'll be glad to accept your suggestions. Just message them to us and we'll put them to work! A copy of this speech will also be available on the page in case you'd like a copy for yourself or to share with someone else.

Before I close, I'd like to say a personal note to all of my close friends who came here today. I didn't ask you to come here in a hope of converting you to Christianity, or in hope of making you feel bad about driving big cars and owning big TVs. I asked you here for two reasons. First, for your support and companionship, which have kept me alive for so long. Second, to let you all know the truth behind the changes you've seen in me and the way I live my life, to let you all know that I've had a very deep, very personal realization about God, about life in general, and to let you know that I will love you all even more regardless of what you choose to believe. I do want your help in this, though. I'll need it. You've already started to help just by being my loved ones, and I hope it will just keep getting better for everyone from here.

I thank you all for your time, and I will pray that my words will stay with you. Just keep an eye out for opportunities to help, and God will shine his blessings on all of us, on all the world! I'm Adam Johnson, and I'm sure this is what God put me here to do. Thank you."

Chapter Seventeen

The Day the Music Died

On January 8, 2009, before daylight, my Son Adam was shot and killed during a mental health crisis, by Officer Christopher Hortness, of the Oklahoma City Police Department, who was the first-responding officer, having been dispatched to Adam's apartment after LeAnn, Adam's former girlfriend called Bryan, Adam's roommate and best friend. Bryan, in turn, had called 911.

Upon arrival, Officer Hortness met Bryan in the parking lot. Upon entering Adam's apartment with Bryan, Officer Hortness found LeAnn sitting on the end of a couch in the living room, to Adam's right, with Adam sitting in the middle of the couch, holding a kitchen knife, with which he had made some shallow cuts on his left wrist. Officer Hortness asked LeAnn to get up off the couch and leave the apartment. She got up, but refused to leave, and walked across the room, to the balcony door. So, Officer Hortness was not able to leave the apartment to give Adam space and time to think, and, in fact, had to step fully inside, to avoid being *"back-lit"* by the outside lighting. He then asked Adam to put down the knife.

Adam then got up, stepped around the end of a coffee table, and took one step forward, while holding the kitchen knife to his side. When he said, *"The only way you're going to get this knife is with your gun,"* Officer Hortness drew his duty weapon and fired four shots. One bullet hit the baseboard in the hallway behind Adam; two bullets penetrated Adam's abdomen; one penetrated his chest. Adam fell to the floor, and was dead within moments.

A second police officer arrived shortly thereafter, and rendered aid to Officer Hortness, who was deeply shaken by the encounter. Adam died lying on the floor of his living room, with two police officers standing over him, neither having the presence of mind to render aid to him after the shooting. EMS arrived a few minutes later, and found Adam to be in full *"asystole,"* with no electrical activity in his heart. They applied CPR, as well as administering epinephrine and atropine, but Adam was gone.

According to Bryan, during the encounter, Adam did not *"charge at the officers,"* as was inaccurately reported by the Press. There was only one officer there at the time of the shooting; the second officer entered the apartment shortly after Adam had been shot. Adam had started walking toward the officer with the knife down to his side. It wasn't a premeditated *"suicide-by-cop,"* but to someone who didn't know Adam, it would look like one. Adam's death was the tragic result of a rash, angry, impulsive statement he made out of shame, embarrassment, and pain. He didn't *"pass away;"* he was killed: victim of a preventable homicide.

At first, we had unanswered questions, which would help us determine whether or not the shooting was largely caused by the officer's procedural errors; but we later found that the officer trying to get LeAnn to leave the apartment. We also found out that, due to not having *"lethal back-up available,"* OCPD officers were prohibited from using their Taser when alone (due to occasional failure of the Taser to effectively incapacitate).

The backup officer arrived moments after the shooting.

Officer Hortness, of course, didn't know Adam, or that Adam would never hurt a fly, let alone a police officer. Officer Hortness acted within policy and protocol. He had arrived there wanting to help; as a result, Adam was dead. It probably would have had a different outcome if Officer Hortness had waited for his back-up to arrive.

To summarize: Adam is dead, partially due to his own mistakes, but mainly due to a long-standing pain and sense of helplessness over his own mental illness, and a snap decision while *"putting his mouth in gear with his brain in park."* Adam died after having been sleep-deprived for over a day, with alcohol in his system, after a cathartic, verbal altercation with a girl he loved, whom he felt had rejected him. He had been drinking for several hours prior to his death.

Alcohol didn't mix well with Adam's medications, and often caused him to act impulsively. It was the alcohol-induced, rash impulsiveness, coupled with Adam's fear of not seeing LeAnn again, that led to his death. He died disappointed in himself, hurting, angry, lonely, and tired. Three days prior, he had been on top of the world, with a bright outlook on his future, as well as his present.

Ironically, he died of loss of blood, on a day that he had made an appointment to donate blood at the Oklahoma Blood Institute. He died cold from blood loss, not covered by a blanket, after days' earlier giving his coat to a homeless man who needed it more than he did. Yet in his final moments, on that blood-stained floor, I know that he was comforted, in the arms of two of God's invisible Emissaries who held him as they told him that God was

155

pleased with him, and was anxious to see him, after moments prior not believing he would ever be successful in finding a life partner. A third angel stood nearby, with his hand on Officer Hortness' shoulder. I *"know"* this because God showed it to me in a vision, as I stood in the living room of Adam's apartment, looking down at the very blood-stained spot where he died.

Adam touched so many people in miraculous ways, and I know he died knowing that he was loved: by God, his parents, family, and friends. He died without doubting his relationship with his Heavenly Father, although, six months prior to his death, he had struggled with questions about God's existence. I know that, because of some most recent passages written by Adam in his own Journal, just a few days prior to his death.

He died with tears in his eyes, which were soon wiped away by the gentle hand of Jesus. Yet, knowing all that...in spite of my own assurance that Adam is now free from pain, fear, and harm...I still hurt more than words can describe. Some days I only want to go be with my Son, but I realize that God has called me to carry on His work, which in a very real sense, was, and is, also Adam's work. It's ironic...I used to wonder whether or not Adam would one day carry on my work here on earth. I wanted that, but it wasn't in God's Divine Plan. He had something different in mind.

Since Adam's death, I have spent a lot of time examining Scripture, in order to figure out whether or not Adam can see and hear what I am doing now. I find little in the Bible, if not nothing, to strongly support this assertion. It seems inconsistent that Adam would be totally without pain, fear, and sorrow if he was to occupy himself by looking down upon my life, and the world around me. If he could see my sorrow, and his Mom's, as well as all of the pain, misery, destruction, and horrible abuses that happen here on earth, he would surely be weeping, rather than enjoying himself.

In the Bible, in the account of the rich man and Lazarus *(Luke 16: 19-31),* it is clear that the rich man could see Lazarus. However, there is nothing there to support that Lazarus could see the rich man. The scripture indicates that unbelievers can see believers in Heaven; not the other way around. That scripture also says nothing about people in heaven seeing people on earth, and what they are doing.

Due to the prognosis connected to Adam's mental illness, his mother and I had previously discussed our concern about how Adam would handle it, if and when either of us died, especially if his mental illness worsened, and he became incapacitated. As it turned out, it was an unnecessary concern. He's in Heaven. We're still here.

I'm reminded of Thanksgiving, 2006, when Adam and LeAnn decided to cook Thanksgiving dinner for Barb and me, in our home in Clearwater, FL. We unwisely had agreed to wash the dishes if they cooked. Their culinary endeavors produced a delicious meal, as well as a colossal mess in the kitchen. We jokingly called our kitchen *"Katrina."* Well, this time, my Son has gone to Heaven, leaving us the mess to clean up. But that's okay.

Chapter Eighteen

Adam Pulled My Pants Down

When Adam was a little guy, he had the cutest little butt. I mean, his face was gorgeous…in fact, when he was a baby, friends of mine on the police department joked that they wanted to borrow him to take to the mall to meet women. His tiny little hands were perfect. He was a very handsome young boy. But as cute as his "north end" was, and all those other parts, I never got over how cute his *"south end"* was. Hey, it's a *"Dad thing."*

When he was old enough to *"go on his own,"* I used to always get tickled whenever I'd take him into a public restroom. He was too short to use the urinal, so he would go into the toilet stall. He wouldn't merely unzip and pull his shorts aside…he'd *"drop trou"* right there, letting his pants and underwear drop to the floor, around his ankles. Being the overly-protective, pedophile-chasing Dad that I was, I'd stand guard behind him, to keep any prospective and curious bad guys from sneaking a glance at my boy's little rear end.

The reason I'm telling you this, is to share with you the first time I knew Adam was still in communication with me, after his death. Saturday, January 10, 2009: Barb and I were driving from Florida to Oklahoma. I had made that trip countless times, each and every prior trip was so wonderfully exciting, because I knew I was going back there to see my Son. This time, though, I was going back to bury him. I was crying as I drove down the road. Barb felt so helpless; unable to find any words to comfort me. Her left hand never left my right shoulder.

On I-10, east of Tallahassee, my eyes began to sting. I

exited the highway, pulled into a *Love's Convenience Store* parking lot, and entered the store. I went into the restroom, blew my nose, and splashed water in my face. I then took a look in the mirror for the first time in over two days. I looked horrible. My face was swollen; my eyes were red from crying. I wanted to die, but I also wanted to pee...and figured I'd better *"go to the restroom"* before further contemplating death in a men's room. Ask any police detective who's investigated a death why I thought that was a good idea; they'll explain it to you.

The one single toilet stall was occupied, and I really had to go. For both safety reasons, cops don't like using public restrooms, particularly urinals. However, due to my bladder's sense of urgency, I resorted to using the urinal, where I pulled my sweatpants and underwear down slightly, and...Voila! My pants AND underwear dropped down to my ankles! I swear, in all my years as a freestanding pee-er, that had never happened. Not once. In fact, it's not happened again, thank goodness, since that day.

As I stood there with my sweatpants and underwear down around my ankles, I immediately thought of Adam as a little boy, standing at the toilet, brandishing his little butt. I began to smile, then laugh uncontrollably....and then to cry again, much to the chagrin of the poor guy exiting the lone toilet stall in the restroom. He looked at me with a combination of confusion, shock, and horror. It goes without saying that he didn't stop to wash his hands. I've never seen someone exit a restroom so rapidly! The next thought in my mind was a fearful one: that I would exit the restroom, to see the man pointing at me, as he described to a deputy sheriff what he had just observed.

Luckily, there was not a *"law enforcement presence"* in that convenience store, at that particular time. I quickly exited the truck stop without being placed under *"citizen's arrest,"* got into our pickup, where I was asked by a very confused and inquisitive wife, *"What's wrong? What happened in there?"* I looked Barb straight in the eye and said, *"Adam pulled my pants down."* She looked at me like I was nuts. Oh well, it's not the first, nor will it be the last time, that I've gotten that look from her.

I knew, though, that something miraculous had just happened. Now, don't get me wrong. I don't actually think Adam did it. He was already at peace, and covered with a thick layer of Joy, basking in Jesus' presence. He was playing *"air harp"* rather than *"air guitar,"* and was entirely too busy groovin' on Heaven to be hanging out in a truck stop men's room pulling jokes on his Dad. No, it wasn't Adam. It was either *"Moe, Larry, or Curly:"* the nicknames I had jokingly given to his guardian angels, long ago. The message was from Adam; the Angel was the Messenger.

Most people, I hear tell, only have one Guardian Angel. Adam, however, needed two-out-of-the-three to be on duty at all times: three during nights and weekends. Man, did those three Celestial Beings earn *their* golden wings here on earth when they were assigned to Adam! Let it suffice to say that, on more than one occasion since Adam's death, when I've needed it the most, Adam has sent them my way to give me an occasional mini-miraculous reminder of how real our Blessed Father is, and how happy Adam is to be where he is, now and forever. Here's another example of how Adam has spoken to me…this time, in a dream, which I wrote about on Facebook, in 2014:

161

Marching Orders

(Dedicated to My Son, Adam)

I had a haunting dream last night...a very different kind of dream than the usual ones I have about my Son, Adam. "Dad, I've got this friend..." are words that I heard on more than a few occasions over the phone, when called by Adam, who died on Jan 8, 2009. Invariably, he was about to put me on the phone with a friend who was in pain or in trouble. While growing up, when staying with me, Adam had spent countless hours sitting near me as I talked to endangered and hurting children and youth on the National Youth Crisis Hotline. He told me once that he told his friends, "If my Dad can't help you through this, no one can."

Last night, I dreamed that Adam came up to me with a little ragamuffin, who appeared to be about ten years of age. Adam began to explain to me how the boy needed help...that he had been abused, neglected, and abandoned, and that he needed me to take care of him. Happy to do so, I agreed...but I was haunted by the distinct impression that Adam was somehow not aware that he had been killed 5 years ago. I felt that I must tell him about how he had died, and so I asked if I could talk to him in private about something important. Adam then went through a doorway, going into the next room, or so I thought. I followed him, and found that he was gone… vanished...leaving me there, with the little boy to take care of.

I recall feeling supremely disappointed that my visit with Adam was cut short, but realized what was most important: taking care of the little child left in my charge by my Son. I can only tell you that, of all the countless dreams I have had about Adam, and dreams with him in them, this dream was different from all the rest. I just can't shake the complicated feelings it evoked. I've been on the verge of tears all day...and, I miss my Son. But now, I've got my "Marching Orders." Time to get up out of bed, and get busy!

Chapter Nineteen

Adam's Obituary

As it appeared in the January 12, 2009 Daily Oklahoman

Adam Joshua Johnson was truly chosen: chosen both by his earthly parents and by his Heavenly Father. Adam now rests with Jesus, after twenty-four years on earth. Born July 31, 1984 in Shawnee, Oklahoma, Adam died January 8, 2009 in Oklahoma City.

A graduate of Edmond North High School and the Academy of Recording Arts in Oklahoma City, Adam was a gifted and versatile musician and Songwriter. As a well-known street musician, Adam played everywhere from the sidewalks of Brick Town in Oklahoma City, to the subways of New York City. From earliest childhood he proved to be a natural-born helper and unselfish giver of himself.

He was a frequent donor at the Oklahoma Blood Institute, participated in street outreach programs for the homeless, and volunteered as a technical consultant for the National Child Abuse Task Force, the National Crisis Intervention Training Institute, and Way Out of the Box. Adam had a heart for God and for helping people, and in spite of his own adversities and challenges, never neglected to help a friend in need or crisis. He regularly attended The Edge Church in Edmond, OK.

He is survived by his Mom, Debra Linville; his Dad, Joel Johnson, his Step Mom, Barb Johnson, his grandparents, Glenn and Joan Alldredge, and his step-siblings, Natalie Gregg and Tim Linville. Other survivors include: Aunt Linda and Uncle Steve Hood, Aunt Diane and Uncle Ed Schmidt, Uncle Ken and Aunt Jeri Johnson, Uncle Dan Alldredge, his cousins, Ian Hood, Paul and Elizabeth Schmidt, Mallory and Jordan Johnson, as well as a host of friends whose lives he touched.

Memorial services will be presided over by his Pastor, Rev. Israel Hogue, and will be held at 2:00 p.m. on Tuesday, January 13, 2009, at Baggerley Funeral Home in Edmond, OK. As a memorial gift in Adam's honor, please give of yourself. Go out and help someone in need today. Adam would have wanted it that way.

Chapter Twenty

Mental Hotfoot #538...What Would Adam Do?

...or...

The Best-Selling Issue of the Daily Oklahoman...Ever!

On the day that Adam's obituary appeared in the Daily Oklahoman, Barb and I went to dinner with my brother, Ken, and his wife, Jeri. After dinner, we stopped at several convenience stores to buy extra copies of the *Daily Oklahoman*, in order to get original copies of Adam's Obituary for family members. For who-knows-what reason, we found relatively few-to-no copies of the newspaper available at each store. After several stops, we pulled into the parking lot of a *7-11* store. Barb volunteered to go into the store to purchase a few copies. She returned a couple of minutes later with four copies. I asked her if that was all they had; she said that there were several more, but that she figured we had purchased enough copies. I disagreed, and exited our pickup.

As I walked into the store, I suddenly thought of the hobby of inflicting *"Mental Hot Feet"* upon total strangers, that had been such a rich source of entertainment for Adam and me. There were six copies of the newspaper still in the rack. I picked up all of them, walked up to the cash register, and placed the papers on the counter, thinking to myself, *"What would Adam do?"* As I looked the clerk in the eye, I said to him, *"I'll bet you've sold quite a few of these today, huh."* The employee replied, *"Well, as a matter of fact, a woman came in here just a couple of minutes ago, and bought four."* I replied, *"I'm not surprised. Everyone is grabbing these because of the coupon. Did you get a bunch of copies for yourself?"*

The clerk responded, *"Uh, no. What coupon are you talking about?"* I replied, *"There is a generic two-for-one coupon in here, good in several stores in the OKC metroplex. If you buy one of ANYTHING, you get two of the same item… free of charge! We're grabbing these up like crazy and selling the coupons for $50 each. I guess the word is getting out, because now everyone is running low."* I continued, *"I'd sell a couple of mine back to you, but they're already spoken for. Look, I gotta go, but, if I were you, I'd text all your friends, right now, and ask them to scarf up as many copies of today's newspaper that they can for you, then go find some more when you get off work. Don't tell them about the coupon, though. They'll take it for themselves.*

But, just to warn you, the coupon is part of a loose insert in the paper, so they're stuck just about everywhere, in several different sections of the paper. You've got to look for them. Text your friends and tell them! Good luck!"

If the word got out, that edition of the *Daily Oklahoman* just might have been the best-selling issue of the year…thanks to Adam. Needless-to-say, my brother Ken and I thought it was hilarious. Our wives, on the other hand, did not. But, as I sometimes explain to my wife, *"you forget, Honey, my sole concern here is my own entertainment, not someone else's. Remember, SOMETIMES I CRACK ME UP!*

Chapter Twenty-One

Adam's Big Send-Off

Prior to the night before Adam's funeral, I had never written out a speech, word-for-word. Nor have I since. On that tragic day, however, it is a good thing that I did, because otherwise, I would have found myself standing there like a blithering idiot, not knowing what to say. I am blessed to still have the written transcript of what I said to the full house at Baggerly Funeral Home. It was a blessing to see the pews packed with friends, relatives, and even people who had never met Adam personally. Most of that horrible day is a blur in my memory, but I DO remember crying and sobbing so hard that I had to stop many times to summon up the strength to continue *Adam's Eulogy*.

Another vivid memory is hearing and seeing all six of the pallbearers (Adam's closest friends) cracking up laughing when I said the word *"Leroy,"* which was one of the key words in the Eulogy. I have placed *Adam's Eulogy* in the Appendices Section of the book (SEE APPENDIX I), and hope that you will take the opportunity to read it. I have tried several times and ways to add it to this manuscript, and even tried to re-type it, verbatim. For some unearthly (probably!) reason, when I do that, it keeps screwing up the page numbers at the bottom of the page, turning this page into page *"1."* Personally, I think Adam sent Moe, Larry, or Curly to play one more *"mental hot foot"* on his dear, old Dad.

Chapter Twenty-Two

Adam's Final Mental Hotfoot: His Big Heart

Throughout his life, from young childhood, until his death, Adam was known for his *"big heart."* He was kind, generous, selfless, loyal, and devoted to his friends and family. Two particular stories come to mind, as I think back on Adam's generous nature. The first one occurred on August 1, 1989, when Adam was 5 years old, staying with me for the Summer in Florida. On Adam's fifth birthday, July 31st, 1989, we spent part of the day at my office at Children's Rights of America, Inc.

I had given Adam some *"projects"* to work on while I was working on a missing child case. The projects consisted of coloring pictures for each of the office staff. He did a very good job of staying quiet and remaining on task. So, I told him that he had done such a good job *"helping Dad,"* that he had earned five dollars, in addition to his birthday money. Wow! Was he excited! He asked me if I would keep it safe for him, along with his birthday money; which I did.

At that time, Jim Bogan, LCSW, served as Clinical Supervisor for the National Youth Crisis Hotline. To this date, Jim and Judy Bogan remain in my cadre of closest and dearest friends. They are like family to me. Jim serves on the Advisory Board of NCITI, Inc. He was particularly helpful to me after Adam's death. Jim has three daughters; Melissa, Allison, and Sara. As a small child, Sara was Adam's *"bestest buddy"* in the world. She was born 364 days before Adam.   To this day, we all look back on Adam's and Sara's preschool years, when they would sometimes fight like cats and dogs while playing with each other, but then cry and throw a fit when it was time for us to leave, and for them to be separated. Adam dearly loved Sara. On her sixth birthday, Jim and Judy held a birthday party for Sara at their home, the day after the office birthday party we had thrown for Adam. We were invited to their home for Sara's party. During the party, Sara received some money in one of her birthday cards: a nice, new, crisp five-dollar bill. At some point during the party, one of the party guests helped him or herself to Sara's five dollars. When the theft was discovered, it was upsetting and heartbreaking to Sarah. Jim and Judy decided to not address the issue by questioning the guests.

Adam saw that Sara was upset, and asked her why she was crying. She told Adam that someone had taken five dollars out of her birthday card. Adam came to me and said he was very sad for Sara, and asked if it was okay with me if he shared his money with her. He decided that he wanted to give her the five dollars he had earned in my office. I was so touched by his tenderness, caring, and generosity, and told him that I couldn't think of a better thing for him to do with his money than to make a friend happy. So, after the party, I took the five dollars out of my wallet, gave it to him, and he took it over to Sarah, handed it to her, and said, *"I'm sad someone took your money. I earned this helping my Dad."*

Let me add one caveat to my description of Adam's lifelong tradition of unselfishness. As a small child, he left it at the door when he entered a MacDonald's restaurant. He would give you all the money in his pocket, and the shirt off his back, but, he wouldn't give up a Chicken McNugget or French fry, if his life depended on it. He guarded those puppies with his life!

Sometimes I would teasingly ask for, or just reach for one. One time when I did that, he laughed and held up a plastic fork, like he was going to stick me in my hand. I laughed, and pointed out that it was I who had bought them for him. He explained, in childlike parlance, that the operative word in that sentence was that they were HIS French Fries and Chicken McNuggets! But, when it came to every other thing that he possessed, he was unselfish.

The second story occurred a couple of weeks prior to his death; a day or so after Christmas, 2008. He was working as a *"Pizza Guy,"* making deliveries for *Pizza Hut* in Edmond, his home town. On a very cold work night in late December, he was wearing a brand new $200 leather jacket that his Mom had given him for Christmas. As he drove the streets of Edmond, delivering pizzas, he noticed a homeless man, standing outside in the cold, next to a building, nearly freezing to death. Adam stopped his vehicle, got out, and gave the man the jacket right off his back.

Since it was well-below freezing outside, he immediately drove to his Mom's house, and told her that he had lost his jacket, asking if he could have one of Don's jackets. Don was Adam's deceased stepfather. Debbie gave Adam a warm coat, and mildly admonished him for losing his jacket. Adam then went back to work. A day or so later, Adam called to confess to me that he had fibbed to his Mom. He had decided to not tell his Mom the truth about the jacket, because he thought she would think that he was not grateful for the gift...when, in fact, he loved it.

Adam felt that a gift of your own possession wasn't much of a gift if that possession didn't mean much to you. He asked me to not tell her about what he had done. I agreed to honor his wishes. To this day, I don't think Debbie actually knows what happened on that night. She will no doubt be aware of it, if she did not already suspect the truth, when she reads this chapter. A little over two weeks after Adam gave his coat away, he was dead, lying cold on the floor of his apartment, bleeding onto the carpet, with the front door wide open, letting in the cold.

Yes, Adam had a big heart; both figuratively and literally. As a final unintended *"Mental Hot Foot,"* I received a copy of Adam's autopsy report, about six weeks after his death. I was stricken by the poetic irony as I read the findings on the physical examination of his body's internal organs.

The average adult male heart weighs approximately 270 grams. Adam had a previously-undiagnosed pathological condition: cardiomegaly. Yes, Adam's heart weighed 440 grams; it was a little over 160% the size of a normal adult male human heart. Since Adam was not an athlete, (non-pathological cardiomegaly is common in athletes), it is entirely possible that, had Adam lived to be older, he could have developed a devastating, perhaps even fatal heart condition later in life, as a result of his anatomic abnormality. *So, as it turned out: Yes, Adam did, after all, "have a big heart."*

Chapter Twenty-Three
Meeting Adam's Birth Family

As previously mentioned, Adam was chosen by God, and by his Mom, and me. To recap the story told in Chapter 6, we brought him home when he was two and a half days old, from our attorney's office. It was a blessed day. Our adoption was private, in that we were told of a birth mother named Andrea, who was pregnant, and financially unable to raise a child. Over time, through a mutual friend, Dr. Sara Nixon, we learned more: that Andrea had withheld news of her pregnancy from the birth father, until she was far enough along to make abortion legally impossible. Andrea was, and is, a Christian, and did not believe in abortion. She feared that, if the birth father knew, he would pressure her to terminate the pregnancy.

So, she carried our Son to full term, and gave birth to him on July 31, 1984. For the next two days, we were on pins and needles, due to a natural fear that she might change her mind, and choose to keep our Son. However, she did not. And you know almost all of the rest of the story, described in Chapters Two and Six. Going forward in time: When Adam was about eight years old, long after his Mother and I were divorced, Debbie visited us one day in our home in Springdale, to explain to Adam about his adoption: how he had been chosen, and how his birth mother loved him so much that she wanted him to be raised by Christian parents who could take good care of him. It was an extremely emotional conversation, but after an initial time of tearful questions, Adam became very much at peace with it. He smiled a big smile, hugged and kissed both of us, then went outside to play with his friends.

Several years later, when Adam was in his early teens, I asked him if he was curious about his birth parents. I told him that, if he ever wanted to find out more, I would try to find more information about his birth family. Years later, when Adam was an adult, I once again breached the subject with him. He told me that he believed that his birth mother had committed an act of love by giving him up, but that, at that time, he was not particularly curious about who she was...that Debbie and I were his Mom and Dad. Over time, I had checked occasionally to see if I could locate Andrea, and learned that her family still lived in the Shawnee area, but that she had moved to somewhere in Texas.

One day, a few months after Adam's death, out of the blue, I felt a sense of urgency to find her, more than I had never felt before. I did a quick name search, and found someone with the same first and maiden names in Burleson, TX. I retrieved a phone number, and two minutes later, I was talking to Andrea Brakebill (her married name). I introduced myself, asked a couple of questions to make sure I had the correct person on the phone, and then broke the tragic news to her about Adam's death. We talked for well over an hour. She shared with me that, after Adam's birth, she had eventually married Adam's birth father, and that they had a second child: a beautiful girl named Kamberly. Shortly after Kam's birth, they divorced. Andrea later got remarried, to a great guy named Gary Brakebill. They had a second child: David. So, as it turned out, Adam has a sister and a half-brother that he never met.

Andrea asked me how far our home was from Lakeland. I told her that, in good traffic, it was about an hour away. She told me that her husband, Gary, was just a few hours away from Lakeland, where he was going to be dropping off a vehicle that he had been hired to deliver. She called Gary, asking him if he would like to meet me, then called me back and said Gary was excited about the possibility. So, I hopped in my car, and drove to Lakeland. Gary was slightly delayed, but by late afternoon, we were sitting in my car, sharing about our respective lives. I told him the story of Adam's remarkable life and tragic death. Gary told me that he needed a ride to the airport or bus terminal to get back to Texas. I called Barb, and asked if she would mind if Gary came to stay with us for a day or two. By that time, he and I both felt like life-long friends. Barb graciously agreed, and Gary and I headed to Clearwater.

Gary spent the entire weekend in our home, and I got to take him on a local sight-seeing excursion. I especially recall watching him take his shoes and socks off, then walk onto Clearwater Beach. It was the first time he had ever visited the Gulf of Mexico. He was thrilled! During that time, it registered with me why the sudden sense of urgency had hit me on that day. If I had delayed calling --even by one day-- I would have missed the opportunity to meet Gary face to face, and to spend that wonderful time with him. To this day, our families have stayed in close touch. As it turned out, Andrea had divorced Adam's birth father, and later married Gary, who was the only real father than Kamberly ever knew. He was a dedicated Christian, and a loving father who loved Kamberly as his own.

Several weeks after Gary and I met, I had the opportunity to travel to Texas to stay with Andrea, Gary, and David. I also got to spend some time with Kamberly, and her new husband, Paden. We had a wonderful visit. The night I arrived in Burleson, I sat with David and Kamberly at Andrea's dining room table, and answered their questions about the brother they had never met. Each time I looked into Kamberly's and Andrea's eyes, I saw Adam...and I still do, each time I look at their photographs.

Gary died on April 14, 2015. I am confident that he now knows and loves Adam on a personal level, as they sit beside each other at the feet of Jesus. Over the years, our two families have remained close: through Adam, we are now an extended family. Now, Adam has met Gary personally. I feel that Kamberly and David are, in a sense, my children, as well...but I would never presume to replace Gary, who will always be their Dad. So, they both call me *"Uncle Joel."* I love them as my own. For over a decade now, Adam has brought us together as one big family, and has kept us together.

Chapter Twenty-Four

Letting Go and Holding On

Since Adam died, I no longer fear death, at all; in fact, I look forward to it. Don't misunderstand me; I am not suicidal…I merely look forward to the moment that I am reunited with my Son, my Mammaw, other loved ones who have gone on before me, and especially, with the Lord Jesus, and my Father God. I have no doubt that I will see my Son again. It has now been a decade plus a year since the most horrible day of my life. I have had two near-fatal car wrecks which, for all intents and purposes, should have killed me. I've nearly lost my right leg from a potentially-deadly bacterial infection. I have overcome skin cancer several times, and yet, here I remain: holding on.

On each of those nearly-fatal occasions, someone said to me that there must be a special reason that I was spared…that God must have a special purpose for me to remain here. I have no doubt that is true. I believe that God has kept me here to continue Adam's legacy, and to fulfill whatever other Divine Purpose God has for me to fulfill on this earth. I have made my peace with this truth. Sometimes, though, I wish that God would hurry up and take me home. I am so tired of the pain and emptiness that only a Surviving Parent can know. I am sick and tired of being separated from my Son, but rejoice in the fact that I confidently know, with a "biblical hope," that I will one day be reunited with him. For now, though, I look forward to continuing to serve God, and to bring hope, healing, and comfort to other Surviving Parents. I especially look forward to the remaining time I have here on earth with my beautiful Blushing Bride, Barb. She is the light of my life; my closest friend. I love her so very much.

I also look forward to continuing to teach, train, and assist helping professionals to do a better job of empathizing, and bringing help and comfort to Surviving Parents. Over the last eleven years, I have been contacted by many Surviving Parents, with whom I have had conversations about the horrific nature and severity of their pain and suffering. I have come to realize that there is so little true understanding of this terrible phenomenon among the many well-intended counselors, therapists, pastors, pastoral counselors, and other helping professionals charged with the awesome and terrible responsibility of ministering to, and aiding the healing within the hearts of parents who have experienced the obscenely-unnatural tragedy of losing a child.

As I mentioned in the beginning of this book: as a veteran police detective, paramedic, and crisis interventionist, I thought I had a good idea of what Surviving Parents endure, and that I understood and empathized with their pain. However, looking back, I realize that I did not have the slightest clue what they were experiencing. Now I do, though. I do not want this responsibility, but I accept it, and consider it a great privilege to serve those suffering families. I can't say I enjoy what I do, but I am blessed and fulfilled by it. My work gives me a sense of purpose.

I believe I am in the advanced final stages of letting go of the many things that I once thought were truly important in life, in order to fully embrace my Calling: I am here to sing Adam's Song, and to make the world a kinder, gentler, more loving place for Surviving Parents who are in need of its healing melody, harmony, and lyrics. Each day I remain here, is another day of letting go, and holding on.

Recently, for the umpteenth time, I entered into a conversation with someone who asked me whether or not I was *"angry at God for taking Adam away."* I shared what I always share: thoughts, feelings, beliefs, and decisions that are reflected in this poem that I wrote in July, 2013. I share why I believe that God did not *"take my son,"* but that I know with confidence that he graciously received him on January 8, 2009.

The following verses, written over six years ago, reflect how I think, believe, and feel today. I want to stress that each suffering Surviving Parent's experiences are unique to them. While I have never felt or expressed animosity toward God for my Son's death, I realize that many parents do feel tremendous anger and confusion about their tragic experience, and seek answers to questions steeped in their own anguish. I also realize that Our Heavenly Father realizes it, as well. He loves and accepts them, and truly understands.

Their difficulty in embracing this Truth, I believe, is often because of some fundamentally-flawed things said to them by well-intended people who should know better, as well as what I believe to be inaccurate interpretations of Scripture. An example is the belief that *"nothing happens that isn't God's Will."* To me, this belief is nonsense. It negates the importance, impact, and purpose of *"Free Will."* I often share with those parents that God understands their feelings, and, judging from my own personal experience, He seeks to comfort and love them, and to give them *"permission to feel."* He has called me to share this message with all who will listen, and to *"comfort the afflicted,"* even if it

181

sometimes involves *"afflicting the comfortable."* Yet, I realize that His Message MUST be gently and patiently shared, rather than critically and aggressively thrust upon others. God knows our pain, and has experienced what Surviving Parents have.

I would give anything to not know this Truth; to be enjoying the sunset of my years here on earth, basking in the love and companionship of my son. But, if Adam were still here, he would probably still be suffering; and, so, I realize that my pain, loss, wants, and desires are largely born out of my own selfishness; because today and forever, Adam now lives in an Eternal Home of Blessed Peace, Joy, and Contentment. He has long forgotten his turmoil here on earth.

> ***"He will wipe away every tear from their eyes, and death shall be no more, neither shall there be mourning, nor crying, nor pain anymore, for the former things have passed away." Revelation 21:4 (ESV).***

I still weep, but Adam's eyes were dried long ago, when the Master gently reached down and wiped the tears from them, looked into the loving eyes of my Son, and said, *"Adam, come in, Son. Your journey of sadness and pain is over; your Eternal Journey with Me has now begun, and will last for Eternity. You now live where there is no pain, fear, or harm. There is also no time here. You did well, my son. In you, I am well pleased."*

I hear God's Voice telling me that, while the music has died for me, the silence is only temporary. If I remain faithful, and listen intently, I can barely hear the faintest hint of God's Miraculous Song in the distance. One day, it will be restored to me for Eternity, if I will only continue to let go, and hold on.

One Day, the Music Will Abound

The music died the tragic day
Three bullets took my Son away.
The light went out; the dark was born
The day I learned to grieve and mourn.

Before that day, I thought I knew
What grieving parents suffer through.
But that great loss could not compare
To any pain that I could share.

My heart became an empty place;
My joy was gone, without a trace.
I thought that peace could only lie
In hope that I would one day die.

But then it came: it was so odd
That I was not *"at odds"* with God.
Because, He understood and knew.
You see, someone killed His Kid, too.

He could have spared Himself the loss
Of Jesus hanging on the Cross.
He could have made all time stand still,
If He'd suspended man's free will.

He could have struck the evil down,
Removed the thorns, and placed a crown
On Jesus' head, and made a slave
Of sinful men He died to save.

And yet, He chose that day to give
His Son, so we could one day live
With Him in Glorious Paradise.
He paid for us a Precious Price.

So, on my knees I choose to pray,
Not, *"Lord, please take the pain away;"*
But for the strength to daily choose
To give my pain for Him to use.

I give my loss, my broken will,
My gifts and skills, so He can fill
Those broken hearts, and wipe the tears;
And soothe the pain, and quash the fears

Of those who weep and need to share
The horrid pain that can't compare
To any other kinds of grief:
The kind that offers no relief.

He did not take my Son away;
Now in His Love, I choose to stay.

Because I know He did receive
My Son, I now choose to believe

That one day I'll be whole again;
My broken heart, my God will mend.
His Gentle Hand will wipe away
All tears, and I'll forever stay

With my Son in a Land of Grace
And Peace. I know God will erase
All mem'ries of my loss and pain,
And in His Home, I shall remain.

For now, I give the emptiness
To God, so He can heal and bless
The hearts of other parents, while
They grieve the loss of their own child.

This simple truth, this precious promise
About the grief that comes upon us:
That when we don't know how to pray,
God's Grace will always let us stay

Inside His Love, safe in His Heart;
And from our lives He won't depart.
He'll stay beside us as we grieve,
If we will trust Him and believe.

But that is easier said than done,
For folks like me who've lost a Son
Or daughter, so please play a part
In helping God heal broken hearts.

The music died that tragic day
Three bullets took my Son away.
For now, I hear the faintest sound;
One Day, the Music Will Abound.

Chapter Twenty-Five

Restored to Significance

I believe that one of Adam's key frustrations was that he falsely believed that his infirmity was a stumbling block to his life having true significance. Nothing could be further from the truth. Through his many gifts of love, caring, and unselfishness, he blessed each and every life that he touched.

"Are they not all ministering spirits sent out to serve for the sake of those who are to inherit salvation?" ...Hebrews 1:14 (ESV)

I believe that funerals are for the living, not the dead, but I also believe that there is an excellent chance that when someone goes to be with God, he or she may receive an update from their Guardian Angel as to who elected to attend their funeral. I choose to believe that Adam was pleasantly surprised, as he received the follow-up report from one of his Guardian Angels, who looked down upon the overwhelming crowd of people who attended Adam's funeral, and saw people there who were Adam's neighbors at the apartment complex where he lived, whom he had not met. They came because of what they heard about him, right after his death.

I know that I felt God's presence on that dark day at Baggerly Funeral Home, so during that darkest hour, I shared with a room full of people about Adam's incredible significance...for my son's benefit. And yet, I was a hypocrite, because, during the weeks, months, and years that followed, I struggled with feelings and beliefs that my life had lost its own significance. For years following his death, I was only a shell of the man I had been while he lived on this earth. I believed that I was no longer Adam's Dad; that I was just an *"Ex-Dad."* Over time, God patiently and gently restored my sense of significance, and made me realize that, unlike many fathers whose Sons carry on in their footsteps, I was walking in his.

"The thief comes only to steal and kill and destroy. I came that they may have life and have it abundantly." John 10:10 (ESV)

Occasionally, the lies planted by *"The Thief"* try to creep back in to my soul; to infect my will, intellect, and emotions, in order to re-instill a sense of hopelessness, despair, emptiness, and loneliness. During those dark times, I try to remember not only to pray (to talk to God), but, more importantly, to meditate (listen to God) after I pray. Once I get back on track, all is usually well. Too many of us make the mistake of not listening after we talk to God. It's like if I asked you a question, then abruptly got up and exited the room before you had a chance to answer. To add insult to injury once more: that's just plain rude, if you ask me.

It is during those times of quiet contemplation that I experience the Truth of God's Significance in my life, and realize that He loves me, has a Special Calling for me, and looks forward to me being reunited with my Son, beyond forever…in a Heavenly Realm where there is no death, no time, no pain, and no sorrow. For now, however, He has more for me to do.

When I need it the most, Adam has one of those Guardian Angels, yet again, *"pull my pants down,"* in one way or another. Each time it happens, he reminds me that he is still with me, and is truly and eternally alive. Here an example:

Chapter Twenty-Six

How I Know Adam is Still Alive and Kickin'

"You've reached the cell phone of Adam Johnson. Adam can't come to the phone right now, but he assures you that if you leave him a message, it will probably irritate him. If you're still listening, hang up. If you can't hang up, leave a message explaining that. Thank you." **(Adam's Outgoing Cell Phone Message at the Time of His Death**)

There are times in every Surviving Parent's life when their day is consumed with the desperate need to believe, to have hope of being reunited with their dead child, and to be assured that their child is happy, at peace, without pain and suffering, and eternally alive. No matter how steadfast their belief that those things are true, doubt and fear sometimes creep in, haunting the Surviving Parent.

I confess that a while back, it had been that way for me, for quite a while...and until that day, I had not shared that with another living soul what I am about to share...and what I originally shared on Facebook... when I found myself in one of those terribly-dark places. I was on the brink of despair, sinking in a quagmire of depression that I just could not shake off. Then, the mailman came to deliver our mail. In the mail box was a piece of physical evidence of what Scripture describes as the manifestation of Faith:

"Now faith is the substance of things hoped for, the evidence of things not seen." (Hebrews 11:1 - ESV)

As an aside, by the way, let me share that every time we have heavy storm clouds, and rays of sunshine burst through, I look up and wonder how magnificent the view is from Adam's perspective...and how Glorious the weather is in Heaven. I often think of that...especially when the Oklahoma weather sucks wind. I share all of that as a preamble to the explanation of a particular piece of mail that I found in my post office box that afternoon that, according to folks at the Post Office, was not possible. I believe it was sent BY Adam, not TO Adam; here's why:

At the time of his death, Adam was living in Oklahoma City, having moved from Edmond. This piece of mail is the only piece of mail I have ever received, addressed to Adam, at my Norman P.O. Box...for one excellent reason: I moved back to Norman approximately four years after Adam died. My PO Box in Norman was NEVER listed as an address for Adam...anywhere. All his mail goes to his Mom's house in Edmond. I suspect that the message, *"The weather is beautiful...wish you were here"* was a special message of reassurance and comfort to me, written in typical Adam-style wit.

Moral of this story: To those of you who do not believe in God, the Afterlife, and in the Supernatural, I don't blame you for being skeptical. But, please understand that, of all people, Surviving Parents believe in *"Hope Eternal"* because they choose to, and more importantly, because they need to. Their faith is a choice...as so is the nonbeliever's lack of faith. Please be slow and careful before you choose to quash a Surviving Parent's faith and hope with the expressed skepticism of your non-belief. Now, take a close look at the piece of *"junk mail"* that awaited me that day.

Oh, and by the way. I have a feeling I know who the mailman was that day: Either Larry, Moe, or Curly.

P.S. Dear Adam: I just got your message, Buddy. And, boy, did I need it! Thank you!

I love you,

Dad

Chapter Twenty-Seven

Adam's Song Continues: A Tribute to Sara Maisano

"The Notes of Adam's Song" is one of the most important programs within the structure of the National Crisis Intervention Training Institute, Inc. This mutual-aid support group consists of special team members who, like me, have experienced the death of a child. We reach out through various media, including, but not limited to: Facebook and other social media sites; our website, *(www.NCITI.org);* our NCITI's Surviving Parents Network, which holds live, online meetings, outreach programs sponsored by local churches; one-on-one contacts; through publicly-offered "Living Tribute" workshops; and via word of mouth. Key members and leaders of the Network are available for outreach services to parents who have lost a child.

Their role is much like a *"Sponsor"* in various 12-Step groups, although the 12-Step recovery model is not incorporated into the Notes of Adam's Song program. None of us who serve as Sponsors for fellow Surviving Parents have, by any stretch of the imagination, *"fully recovered"* or *"arrived at our destination."* We recognize our recovery as a continual process. We are merely fellow travelers on a dark and windy road, a bit farther along than those we help. In helping them, we are helping ourselves.

One of the members of NCITI's Governing and Advisory Boards is Jim Maisano, a very good friend and colleague, who recently retired as Assistant Chief of Police of the Norman Police Department, where I served from 1979 through 1984. Jim and his wife Alicia raised three children. One of their daughters was Sara Maisano, a beautiful young woman who was savagely murdered by the estranged boyfriend of one of Sara's closest friends. Sara died a courageous, yet brutal and senseless death, while successfully and bravely fighting to save the life of her friend. Her murderer is now serving a life sentence, without possibility of parole, in the Oklahoma state penal system.

I sat with Jim, Alicia, their daughter Melissa, and the rest of the family, during two court hearings, as well as the sentencing of the monster who took Sara's life. He *"took a plea,"* in order to avoid the death penalty, which he most-richly deserved. On both occasions, I looked into the cold, cruel, contempt-filled eyes of the man who murdered Sara, as he perused her parents and family with a stark look of scorn on his face. I was stricken by his apparent lack of remorse, and the stark contrast between his soulless gaze, and the warm, smiling, and loving eyes of his victim.

While on earth, Sara had an exceptional affinity toward animals...especially those who were homeless, abused, and endangered. She devoted a significant amount of time rescuing and caring for them. Her tender heart and dedication to those innocent, vulnerable creatures now live on. In her honor and memory, a special sanctuary for discarded dogs and cats was established, as a living monument to her life.

I never had the honor of meeting Sara. As a small token of my posthumous love for her, I wrote the following poem. In addition to its entry into this book, Sara's poem is also included in one of my poetry anthologies, entitled, *"Tributes."* **To Jim and Alicia: May God continue to comfort you in the empty, horrible void that lies within your hearts, due to the death of your precious Sara.** This poem is for Sara, and for you:

You'll Take That Puppy for a Walk

(Dedicated to Sara Maisano and Her Beloved Family)

I didn't know you on this earth,
But knew your Dad before your birth.
We served together *"way back when,"*
And now, Dear One, I call him *"Friend."*

I also have the joy to know
Your precious Mom, who loves you so;
As well as Trent, who has steel nerves,
As he, like Dad, protects and serves.

Melissa's in my heart, as well.
She loves you; I know you can tell.
She misses you, and prays each night
That God will always hold you tight.

Through them, I've come to love you, too.
My heart breaks o'er what you went through.
When your cold killer came to trial,
I sat there with your parents, while

The judge sent Thompson on his way
To never see the light of day.
I sat there and looked in the eyes
Of that cold monster, and despised

His heartless, senseless coward's act.
I know, Dear One, this truthful fact:
That Justice will be met some day
When he does cower, weep and pray

For mercy, but will not find peace;
His pain and torment will not cease.
Remorse was not what he displayed,
On his face cruel hatred stayed.

It struck me how his ugly soul
Was like a black, consuming hole;
So different from your shining light,
That brightened up the darkest night.

Our world was kinder, gentler, Child,
When you were in it, undefiled.

And Heaven's now a Better Place,

Since you moved in, Sweet Child of Grace.

My Son lives there; I hope you've met.

When you died, I asked him to get

With you, and show you all around.

I hope, with him, that you have found

A puppy who lives in the air;

Now free from hunger and despair.

I hope when you and Adam talk,

You'll Take That Puppy for a Walk.

Copyright 2013, Joel Johnson

Chapter Twenty-Eight

NCITI's Programs and Services for Surviving Parents

The National Crisis Intervention Training Institute was founded in 1996, originally under the name of the *"National Child Abuse Task Force."* Over the next decade, as the organization's scope of services changed and expanded, the name changed, as well. Beginning as an organization that addressed child exploitation, abuse, and neglect-related training issues, NCITI now focuses on an array of issues related to various crises involving exploitation, abuse, and catastrophic loss.

A decade ago, about a year after Adam's death, I started designing specialized services which are specifically directed to aiding Surviving Parents. The following are some of the services and resources which are available to surviving parents, those who care for them, and for investigators and helping professionals who provide direct services to Surviving Parents:

Community Seminars and Training Courses

NCITI currently offers 38 training courses for law enforcement and helping professionals, including clinicians, social workers, pastoral counselors, grief and bereavement counselors, and crisis interventionists. For a comprehensive list of available course titles, go to our website: **www.NCITI.org,** and click on the *"Available Training"* page. There you will find training courses which may be requested by local agencies and organizations, as well as churches, synagogues, and mosques. In addition to training for professionals, the website lists several brief community-based seminars which are offered at local venues, for a *"love offering."*

Surviving Parents Network

NCITI's *Surviving Parents Network* is a mutual-aid support group for surviving parents and those who care for them. Live, weekly online meetings are held, connecting attendees with each other in a safe, confidential environment. To learn more about the group, and to request a link to attend these free meetings, please contact me at ***JJohnson@NCITI.org.*** After a brief screening interview, you will be notified of available meeting times and dates. This format allows people all over the country to participate in the meetings, at no financial cost. Members may elect to provide a small donation to help offset the operating costs of NCITI's programs. However, donations are not required, but are appreciated.

Each meeting consists of mutual aid support for Surviving Parents, as well as open forum discussion of an array of relevant topics, including, but not limited to:

- *Risk to Surviving Parents' Marriages.*
- *Danger Signs of Complicated Grief.*
- *First Response to Suicidal Emergencies.*
- *How to Travel the Road to Recovery.*

The Living Tributes Workshop

Offered in both live-online and live-workshop formats, this special event leads Surviving Parents in creative exercises focused on assisting them in developing a living legacy project, honoring their deceased child.

www.NCITI.org Website

The NCITI workshop provides various free tools, as well as technical guidance, to empower Surviving Parents, and to aid them in the recovery process. Some of those resources may be found in the *"Free Forms and Resources"* at www.NCITI.org.as well as other sections of the website.

The Notes of Adam's Song Program

As discussed elsewhere in this book, there sometimes exists the need for direct contact with Surviving Parents on a 1:1 basis. Within the *Surviving Parents Network* is a select group of Recovering Surviving Parents who are especially trained by NCITI to operate in a *"Sponsor"* capacity, for Surviving Parents who are early-on in the recovery process. Currently, there are only a handful of qualified Sponsors. Recruitment, screening, and training of Sponsors is under development at the time of this book's publication. If you are either interested in becoming a Sponsor, or are needing one, contact me at my email address: **JJohnson@NCITI.org.**

NCITI's Psychological Autopsy Team

Ironically, at the time of Adam's death, I was working on developing a uniform method of conducting *"Psychological Autopsies,"* to be used in undetermined death investigations. The issues that I faced were:

• Many cases of death by other-than-natural causes present circumstantial evidence which may indicate more than one possibility as to manner and cause of death, leading to an *"undetermined"* finding. While medical autopsies render findings that may lead to a medical opinion, conventional forensic methods are sometimes bound by limitations.

• Conventional investigative methods often help to determine *"who, what, when, where, and how"* co-factors of the death in question. Outside the realm of forensic pathology, however, often lies the question of *"Why"* to be answered, especially when using victimology as a detection tool to identify at large *"UnSubs"* (Unknown Subjects).

• Psychological autopsies help to resolve the *"why"* question, but due to reasons to be discussed, they sometimes do not enjoy equal weight of scientific certainty commonly attributed to forensic medical autopsies. NCITI is working to overcome that limitation. Therefore, I determined that there was a need for a uniform, evidence-based, scientifically-recognized methodology for conducting psychological autopsies. I developed comprehensive methods for a conventional psychological autopsy, and a *"Therapeutic Psychological Autopsy,"* which would overcome obstacles which have historically blocked uniform recognition in the scientific, legal, law enforcement, and medical communities.

I designed protocols to be practiced by a special inter-disciplinary investigative group within NCITI's *Critical Incident Response Team,* with the goals of confirming or verifying causes and modes of death, co-morbidity contributors, as well as probable motivational intent, in equivocal cases involving undetermined, suspected, or forensically-confirmed death by means of accidental, suicidal, or homicidal causes.

I developed a team structure consisting of a Chief Field Forensic Investigator, a Case Assignment / Intake Specialist, and a Case Manager / Aftercare-Volunteer Coordinator, in addition to paid and professional-volunteer team members such as a crisis intervention specialist, certified addictions counselor, grief &

bereavement counselor, licensed clinical social worker, physician specializing in addictions and pain management; clinical psychiatrist / neurologist; forensic psychologist; pediatrician; attorney; pastoral counselor; clinical psychologist, and a veteran homicide investigator.

In *"Therapeutic Psychological Autopsies,"* special aftercare services are designed to be extended to family members and *"Significant Others"* of the Decedent, to aid those individuals for a significant period of time following the death of their loved one. I developed an extensive training program for law enforcement officials, as well as other members of the Psychological Autopsy Team, as well as a Training Manual which could be utilized by various specialized professionals.

Ironically and tragically, Adam's case was the first case in which I incorporated the NCITI Psychological Autopsy methodology. In that flagship case, many of the protocols were refined and modified, to form the current team approach utilized by NCITI's Psychological Autopsy Team. This is yet another way in which Adam's death served to aid family members of other Decedents, and to pave the way for innovative investigative methods which have since been adopted by many police departments throughout Oklahoma. For more information on this special program, readers may go to the www.NCITI.org website, or may email me at ***JJohnson@NCITI.org.***

SPECIAL NOTE:

For further description and explanation of the NCITI Psychological Autopsy process, see APPENDICES I-IV, at the back of this book.

Chapter Twenty-Nine

Is It Too Late?

I am blessed to remember so many things about the last day I spent with Adam here on earth...as well as our last conversation, three days before his death. Both were wonderful experiences, full of love, humor, and mutual respect. In contrast, I sometimes have the sad experience of visiting with Surviving Parents whose last words with their departed child were not pleasant; filled with memories that will cause them permanent regret and torment. This poem is for them, it's called:

Of Roses Red and Sweet Wine Days

An age-old topic of debate:
"Once they are gone, is it too late?"
When grief is pierced by shining hope,
How can we ever learn to cope

With all our pain and all our fears?
We learn to take our precious tears,
And turn them into sweetest wine;
To quench the thirst within our mind.

But while I have the Joy to know
That my last times with my Son showed
Him, without doubt, that he was loved,
I pray to My Sweet Lord Above

To place a Hand of Peace upon
The heads of parents who have gone
With deep regret and harsh remorse,
Upon a sad, most-tragic course

That their relationships did take.
For those poor souls, my heart does break,
Because they feel such guilt and pain.
I pray that they will lose the stain

That tarnishes their mem'ries of
Their time with children whom they love.
I pray that they might find a way
To wash the guilt and shame away.

Those parents yearn for peace, and yet,
If buried deep in harsh regret,
The wine and roses cannot heal
The horrid pain that they oft feel.

So, when their darkest mem'ries grow
Like roses red in whitest snow,
They're robbed of beauty in their lives,
As thorns pierce them like sharpened knives.

And so, they languish in their pain,
Filled with regret, and oft remain

In misery, in darkened days;
Forgotten peace: it never stays.

Our grief recovery oft depends,
On how we overcome "loose ends."
The harshest pain a parent feels
Is when the death of their child steals

The life from deep within their heart;
Their very soul is torn apart.
My Precious God oft says to me
These words that have helped set me free:

"Please trust, dear Joel; know that I
Have wiped the tears from Adam's eyes.
Your child now knows My Joy and Peace;
His time with Me shall never cease."

"With a now-perfect mind he knows
That you love them and miss him so."
And while those words don't stop the pain,
I can, at least, go forth again.

For you who do not know the joy
Of sweet peace with your girl or boy,
I pray that you will someday see
That self-forgiveness is the key.

So, make amends in your own way.
I pray your child will always stay
In constant contact with your heart;
And from your life will n'er depart.

I pray, my friends, God's Peace you'll know,
And through your hearts will always flow
Those mem'ries of a love that stays:
Of Roses Red, and Sweet Wine Days.

Copyright 2014, Joel Johnson

Chapter Thirty

A Change of Hearts Begins with Me

Lately, I've been meditating about how flawed we all are, and how little mercy and understanding we tend to show others, while at the same time feeling frustrated when people do not show us mercy, and/or misunderstand us. Some recent events reminded me of a poem I wrote seven years ago, which was inspired by a painful experience in my past; one that happened on one of many times in my life when I have been tempted to cast the first stone. It would not be appropriate for me to say that I hope you enjoy this poem...but I do hope it speaks to your heart.

A Change of Hearts Begins with Me

One day, I sat and listened to
Some *"righteous folks"* I barely knew
Discuss, with venom, a poor lad,
Whose plight on earth was truly sad.

But, while they could have eased his pain,
They chose, instead, to wound and stain
His reputation; now it's lost.
Their entertainment had great cost.

With loving words, they could have healed.
Perhaps that young lad would have kneeled
And thanked the Lord for showing love,
Through Emissaries from above.

But, due to their snide, mocking tone,
A suff'ring boy now bears his own
Despair and pain, because he knows
That no one cares about his woes.

He knows that others deem him *"bad."*
My heart wept for that hurting lad.
I prayed that God would call and send
A true believer who would end

The awful lie that boy believes;
The horrid lie that man receives
Into his heart when in a lurch:
That he can't trust God's Holy Church.

I'd grown so tired of people who
Stand ready to do great harm to
Someone whose life is not the same.
I'd grown to shun those men who blame;

Who hold themselves above the rest,
And, who avoid this simple test
Of worthiness to cast a stone:
"Let every man think of their own

Transgression as they grab a rock,
And throw it as they jeer and mock.

For, if some guilt they do not know,
The sacred right is theirs to throw

Those deadly, hard stones, if they can
Say 'sinlessness' applies to them."
I'd grown so tired of hearing men
Are guilty of some "special sin."

When, actually, this God-born fact
Condemns each harsh, judgmental act:
"All men have sinned, and thus have failed
The Will of God" that has prevailed

Since Adam and his mate walked out
Of Paradise with painful shouts
Of shameful guilt, and sad regret,
For their own sinfulness; and yet:

We are so staunch, and do not budge,
Because we deem ourselves as Judge
And Jury, as we aim to blind
And wound our fellow, suffering kind.

We are together in this place.
We're all in need of Precious Grace
Of God, who sent the ONLY man
Whoever walked the earth and can

With righteousness so truly say,
"I came to take your sin away.
I don't condemn, I do not store
Your guilt, so go and sin no more."

I lashed out at those wicked men
Who wallowed in their own foul sin.
I turned my eyes, and kept my gaze
Upon their sinful, wicked ways.

I gave them hell, and told them that
A Righteous God on His Throne sat;
For their eternal fate I feared.
By then, the boy had disappeared.

I looked around, until past dawn,
To find where that poor boy had gone.
I heard that he had left our town.
That wretched boy was never found.

At first, I was so angry at
The men who in harsh judgment sat.
Because they had distracted me,
And, now the boy would not be free.

The day I heard those *"hypocrites,"*
I prayed to God, who gloriously sits

Upon His Throne, then realized,
As scales fell from my blinded eyes.

I saw myself before a Bench
Of Judgment, then smelled MY own stench.
I realized I, too, was stained;
That I had also judged and blamed

Those *"hypocrites,"* but it was me
Who God had called to heal and free
That hurting lad, but I'd instead,
Cast stones at other brothers' heads.

I searched for days, but could not find
That hurting lad who haunts my mind.
I've prayed that God will bring a friend,
So, all his pain and strife will end:

A friend who will relieve the pain,
And help that hurting lad regain
A sense of love, and peace, and grace,
And put a smile upon his face.

A friend who can explain why folks
Reduce their faith to hurtful jokes;
That we are ALL imperfect men,
Who need God's Grace to cleanse our sin.

I may not ever see that boy,
Or share with him my blessed joy.
That is a thorn that I must bear,
To daily teach me how to care.

For now, the Lord will Comfort me.
I pray that one day I will see
That lad, and know that he is loved:
Embraced by Our Great God Above.

I'll not forget, now that I've learned;
Upon my mind his face is burned.
I claim by faith that God will bring
Another chance to share the King

With that poor lad who never had
A single moment to be glad
That he had met a man like me.
I pray that his heart will be free.

I felt so bad for him that day,
But judgment stole my gaze away.
I took my eyes off God's Own Son;
Distracted by the wicked one.

If we would only live each day
By asking God to take away

Our tendency to judge and shame,
To fail to love, to harm, and blame.

Then, we might see a better world;
One where God's Blessings are unfurled;
A kinder, gentler, better place
Where all who live there know His Grace.

God's humbled me, and showed me how
To bring about His Kingdom now:
By focusing, not on the lies,
But keeping focused on the Prize.

He placed into my heart a Voice
That gives to me a blessed choice
To give my life, my words, my deeds,
So, He can meet the sufferer's needs.

I've learned love's more than what we feel.
It's how we comfort, give, and heal.
I've learned that healing truly starts
When God's Love brings a change of hearts.

So, now, I pray to serve, each day,
My God, who washed my sins away;
To set the wretched captives free,
A Change of Hearts Begins with Me.

Chapter Thirty-One
There Is No Toxin like Regret

There are seven things that I am grateful for, in light of Adam's death:

•   I cannot recall any significant conversation that I ever had with Adam during his entire lifetime, when I did not end the conversation by telling him that I loved him.

•   Our last day which we were together physically (6 months prior to his death) was, as I have described it before, "a perfect day, except for one thing: it didn't last forever."

•   My last earthly conversation with Adam, which occurred three days prior to his death, was a very bright, positive one, rife with humor, joy, and warmth.

•   Adam and I enjoyed an extraordinarily close relationship, with virtually not a single day of estrangement in our twenty-four years together here on earth.

•   God has given me the privilege to *"get outside of myself,"* and to find purpose, meaning, and significance in my life.

•   In light of what we have been able to accomplish in the last decade, Adam's extraordinary life and tragic death did not happen in vain. I do not believe that Adam's death was God's Will.   I do not believe that God took Adam away from us. I believe that God Graciously Received him into Heaven, and that He has chosen to use *"Adam's Song"* to facilitate recovery and healing for many, many Surviving Parents.

•   There is absolutely no doubt in my mind and heart as to where Adam is today and forever: an Eternal Home with Jesus, where I will one day be reunited with him, in a land where there is no time, death, suffering, tears, or regret.

In my adventures over the last eleven years, I have encountered Surviving Parents who are far less fortunate than I. I have listened to tearful accounts of instances where parents turned their backs on their children, prior to losing them, forever. Many have told me of months, and even years when there was a total lack of contact with their children, and where their children were deemed *"persona non grata,"* long before their earthly demise.

In some of the most graphically-painful accounts by parents who now feel doomed to a lifetime of remorse and regret, I have been told of the last words they said to their now-dead child, and that they would give their very life to be able to go back in time to change what they did or said. Upon occasion, I have the opportunity to speak to parents of estranged children who are still living on this earth, but about whom a parent has described as, *"dead to me."* I take every available opportunity to heed warning, and to strongly encourage those individuals to reach out to their estranged child, while they still can. Sometimes it works; sometimes it does not.

A few years ago, I had the privilege of getting to know a remarkable young man named Jonathan Allen, who came into national acclaim as a contestant on *America's Got Talent*. During his audition, Jonathan shared the most painful experience of his life: When asked if his parents were supportive of his pursuit of music, Jonathan shared that his adoptive parents –self-professed devout Christians-- had disowned him, and kicked him out of their home on the night of his eighteenth birthday…because he is gay. This disclosure broke the hearts of America. It certainly broke mine.

I was deeply moved by Jonathan's situation, and wrote a poem in his honor; a poem which included a direct message to his parents. Soon afterward, the opportunity arose for me to reach out to Jonathan, to get to know him personally, and to share with him about Adam's remarkable life. I shared the poem, *"America's Adopted Son,"* with him, as well as with one of his sisters. Since that day, my prayer has been that, before it is too late, his parents will realize the hypocrisy and sinfulness of their decision --born out of their own dogmatic beliefs—will repent, and reach out to their son, in an effort to reconcile with him, and restore the relationship which God intends and wants them to enjoy.

It has been over six years since I sent the poem to Jonathan. To date, he is evidently still *"dead"* to his parents. I recently was able to share this poem with his sister, with whom Jonathan still has a close relationship. Even so, however, I pray that other parents who are in similar situations, will read this book, and become restored with their estranged children. The next poem is dedicated to him.

America's Adopted Son

(To Jonathan Allen -- America's Got Talent 2013 Finalist)

Astounded at the hearts he's won,
America's Adopted Son
Has now begun to comprehend
As his soul has begun to mend.

New family replaced the tears;
New confidence replaced the fears,
As he stood up before the crowd,
And millions cheered him strong and loud.

When he sang *"Time to Say Goodbye,"*
I bowed my head; began to cry.
For one brief moment, as he sang.
Sweet thoughts of fondest memories rang

Like chapel bells in autumn air.
It was just then my heart did tear
Apart as I thought of the plight
On that boy's eighteenth birthday night

When he was told to leave his home
With broken heart, he then did roam.
And yet, he did not label them;
He only shared of chances grim

That they would ever hold his hand;
Or hug his neck, or change their stand.
And yet, this lad, but a small child,
Was handed to them undefiled.

In eighteen years, they did discard
A treasured gift put in their charge.
Then two years later, he stood tall
Upon a stage in a great hall,

Before four judges and a crowd;
Before one verse the crowd grew loud
And rose up to their feet and cheered.
Rejection that the lad had feared

Was now a thing of distant past.
The feelings felt will always last.
His strength and grace filled hallowed air.
He more than entertained, he shared

His pain, his life, his sense of joy.
He captured us, that blessed boy.
He stole the hearts of those who wept,
Within their prayers his soul was kept.

As people heard his precious gift,
His smile appeared, his fear did shift

To new-found, strengthened confidence.
His entire world has now changed since

The beauty of his precious soul
Began to heal; to make him whole.
For it was more than mere applause
That worked a miracle, because

He also heard that he belonged;
That others cared that he was wronged
By those who gave him up because
Of what they deemed as *"God's Strict Laws."*

Ironic they should feel that way,
And also preach their soul will stay
In God's Hand, and that nothing can
Steal them away from Promised Land.

They claim Adoption by the Lord.
I pray their sight will be restored,
And that they realize THEIR sin;
That healing will one day begin

By taking logs from their own eyes,
While in another, splinters lie.
Adopted children, after all,
Show us that God will always call

Out to His children; Love will stay
Within their hearts, and find a way
To bring them Home, because He loves
Them as much as His Son Above.

I offer this to those who shun
America's Adopted Son:
I pray your judgment soon will shift
And that you won't lose God's Great Gift.

Your Son has one burning desire:
To reach through thick and twisted mire;
To take your hand; to be restored.
He loves you all; he loves the Lord.

You don't have to agree with him,
But if you shun, your chance is slim
Of having peace of heart restored,
Because you have, before the Lord,

Condemned the debtor, after God
Forgave your debt; I find that odd.
You're missing out on blessings great.
Please call your Son; please do not wait.

And now, to you, Sweet Precious Lad:
I want to tell you I am glad

And proud to be a special part
Of healing your once-broken heart.

I offer this, before I'm done…
Important Lesson Number One:
You're much more than a gorgeous voice.
Eternally, you are God's Choice.

If you could not a single note
Belt out, you'd have His Precious Vote.
His Love for you does not rely
Upon your acts, or how you try

To earn His Love, It's not His Plan.
You're safe within His Mighty Hand;
Not for your talent. Your true worth
Comes from His Choice since your first birth:

To give to you His Precious Prize;
To look in to your smiling eyes,
And say to you, His Chosen One:
"You're also MY Adopted Son."

Copyright 2013, Joel Johnson

And, here is yet another message for suffering Surviving Parents who may be tortured by the most bitter of swills: *Regret.*

By Drinking From His Cup of Hope

There is no toxin like regret;
It poisons hurting souls, and yet,
Propelled by pain we rush to fill
Our cups with that most bitter swill.

These useless words we often say:
"If I could go back to that day;
Oh, wouldn't it be so sublime
If I could just go back in time?"

The truth, however, is that we
Can't cast our eyes ahead and see
The future, if our yesterday
Consumes us as we while away

In dark, foreboding guilt-wrought pain;
Our peace devoured by our self-blame.
We must learn how to pierce the night
By looking to tomorrow's light.

I hate *"Time Bandits,"* for they take
Our peace as we oft lie awake.

Condemned by self, we dwell upon
Mistakes and tragedies long-gone.

We must learn to embrace our past;
To grow from it, but then, long last,
Tuck it away, and venture forth
To find how much our future's worth.

Then, we can finally find God's Peace:
A Perfect Hope that shall not cease.
Our past is gone, so let's not waste
The sweetest lessons we might taste

When God converts our bitter shame
Into a drink free of self-blame;
More sweet than wine, we'll learn to cope
By Drinking From His Cup of Hope.

Chapter Thirty-Two

Special Lessons for Those Who *"Mean Well"*

Awhile back, I was talking to a friend on Facebook, who is a fellow Surviving Parent. We were discussing people who come across as overtly-religious when speaking to someone who has lost a child. The subject came up because she had recently *"unfriended"* someone on Facebook who (although well-intentioned, I'm sure) had come on entirely too strong a while back...in a zealously- religious way. My friend describes herself as being *"more spiritual than religious."*

I care about her, and mourn with her. She has lost two children: One to suicide, and another to an accidental overdose. My Son was killed, yet I don't know exactly how she feels. I understand her pain to the point that another Surviving Parent can, but her grief is unique to her, and is compounded by losing two children instead of one. I try to be supportive, and I do pray for her and her family when they request it. I choose not to be overtly religious when I talk with her, and to pray for her in silence.

That is my policy and practice with all grieving parents...unless they breach the subject first, and initiate conversation about religion. I do that because I know how risky religious rhetoric can be in those situations, and I NEVER want to close a door before that suffering person invites me to walk through it. I have never been angry at God for Adam's death, but I understand why some parents are. I also believe that God understands, and that those parents' anger is okay with Him, too. Oft times, well-meaning people in that situation say things that are unintentionally hurtful, such as *"We can't always understand*

227

God's Will," "God needed another angel in Heaven, so He took
_____," "The Lord giveth, the Lord taketh away," "We can't always
understand God's Will," et cetera.

Each of those statements and questions have the potential
to deeply hurt a Surviving Parent, and to alienate them from God,
at a time when they may need God the most. For example, *"We
can't always understand God's Will"* implies to many people that
God was either the perpetrator of the child's death, complicit in
the child's death, was unaware or did not care, was powerless to
prevent it, or simply did not care enough about it to pay attention
or to respond.

"But, Joel," you may be thinking, *"A parent who has just
lost a child needs the Word."* While this is a valid point, let me
offer this: In comedy, timing is everything. In a catastrophic
situation such as death of a child, timing is also vitally important.
Jumping into *"nouthetic (scriptural) gear"* too quickly may slam
a door shut before you have the opportunity to walk through it.

My recommendation to any of you reading this, is that
whether or not you're a Christian, don't preach in those situations;
just love the person, and say: *"I can't begin to imagine your pain.
I feel so helpless yet I don't know what to say. If I could take your
pain away, I would. I don't know what to do, other than to be here
for you. I love you, and my heart is broken for you. I'm here for
you, no matter what. I love you."* I also recommend you pray for
discernment and wisdom, and venture gently into this delicate
area. Remember, the suffering, Surviving Parent may be feeling
ambivalence or even hostility toward God. You are God's first
line of ministry at that critical time. Be prepared emotionally, as

well as spiritually, and proceed with caution. Love and tenderness speak louder than words.

God will use those words to do more healing than a million Bible verses and religious platitudes. As they acknowledge the magnitude and unique nature of the suffering Surviving Parent's pain, they also assure them they are not alone. When, and if, the time comes to speak about religion, or to share Bible verses, the suffering person will let you know, believe me.

To my friend who was bothered by the religious overtones of the well-intended person: I love you. To the well-intended person who was *"unfriended"* because of what you meant to be healing and helpful, I am confident that you meant well. Your intentions were good. I know you, too, have suffered greatly, as well. You remain in my prayers.

On another note, to those who have a tendency to be critical and harsh, however, and are coming from a position of judgment, I have written the following poem:

Sticks and Stones

(Directed Toward Harsh Critics of Surviving Parents)

The man who said *"while sticks and stones*
Break bones, words are not bad,"
Did not know how a parent moans
Because a child is sad.

He did not know that in their love
They'd die to save their kin
From all the evil God above
Hates most, and deems as *"sin."*

He didn't how many try
To shelter and to spare,
But even though they often cry,
It's not enough to care.

In spite of how they work and slave
To do their very best,
Sometimes they can't rescue and save
Their children from the rest

Of all the things that lurk and hide
In this big scary world.
They cannot always stem the tide
As danger is unfurled.

Because, in spite of what they do
To shelter and make whole,
Their little ones are people, too,
Each with a willful soul.

I write this verse to those who blame;
To those so-called *"experts,"*
Whose *"counsel"* brings more pain and shame;
Whose *"wisdom"* wounds and hurts.

Your words are logs and boulders thrown,
So please do pause and pray,
Before you open your big mouth
And take their Peace away.

How would you like it if some fool,
Who did not have the facts,
Assumed that your parental rule
Caused all your children's acts?

How would you like it if your pain
And loss were made much worse
By words that damage, warp, and stain?
Please Take to Heart this Verse.

Copyright 2014, Joel Johnson

The Top 10 Things to NEVER Say to a Surviving Parent

Number 10: *"Oh, really? How terrible! I'm sorry to hear that! How'd it happen? What made him/her do it?"*

• Response: At the crucial juncture of your first notification, it's NOT important that you know the gory details. What IS important is the suffering survivor know that you are focused on their needs…not your *"need to know."*

Number 9: *"At least he/she didn't suffer. My cousin's child died of leukemia. It took him over a year to die. It can always be worse. You're blessed that he went quickly and painlessly."*

• Response: This is just SO wrong on SO many levels: Catastrophic, sudden losses can be even more immediately impacting than chronic losses. Redirecting to someone else's tragedy can give the impression that you're minimizing the suffering survivor's loss. You don't have all the information on how long, or severely, the victim suffered. The suffering survivor is extremely unlikely to see any part of their tragic loss as a *"blessing."*

Number 8: *"I know how you feel. My __ died last year."*

• Response: You DON'T know how they feel. No two people suffer the same. Many dynamics of a familial relationship (co-factors and co-morbid factors) may affect the type, magnitude, severity, and longevity of the grieving/mourning process. Again, this response is also redirecting focus away from the suffering survivor's loss, back to someone else's (yours).

Number 7:   *"It's been __ years. It's time you got over it and got on with your life."*

•   Response: Death of a child is something a Surviving Parent NEVER *"gets over."* Sanctioning, estimating, and/or expecting time lines for recovery is inappropriate and unrealistic. Remember…some people remain outside their grief for years, prior to working through, or even beginning the healing process.

Number 6:   *"At least you have other children. Some people don't, you know."*

•   Response: Regardless of whether or not a parent has other children, the death of a child creates an ever-empty, un-fillable hole in their heart and their life. The parents' responses to their child's death can also pathologically affect their relationships with their other children.

Number 5:   *"Don't blame yourself."*

•   Response: While guilt is something we feel, and blame is something we do, these terms are often interchangeable in the minds and hearts of Surviving Parents, and must be addressed. Telling them to not feel something --or to take responsibility for something they feel guilty about-- invalidates their feelings, impeding their self-perceived entitlement to their own feelings (their *"right to feel."*)

Number 4:   *"Don't feel that way /Don't say that! You were a perfect parent!"*

•   Response: Again…wrong on so many levels: It

233

takes away their right to feel. It takes away their right to communicate their thoughts, feelings, fears, guilt, and remorse. They were NOT perfect parents. No one is. No matter how excellent they were at parenting, they have SOME regrets. It is natural to feel that, no matter how good a parent you were, you somehow could have/should have done something to save your child. Within this "feelings pit" swims the emotional predators *"Should have," "Could have," "What if," and "If I had only..."*

Number 3: ***"Time heals all wounds. It will get better over time."***

•   Response: Over time pain may or may not be deadened or dulled, but that is not the same as wounds being healed. Tragic losses of the magnitude of losing a child may be integrated into a Surviving Parent's life, but it is something he/she never "gets over." It is common for early-onset emotional, psychological, cognitive, and spiritual reactions to recur, even years after losing a child.

Number 2: ***"Was he/she a Christian? Good. Then at least he's in a better place. God needed another angel in Heaven."***

•   Response: Very dangerous ground. While this may be true, and a source of comfort to parents who are Christians, beware of emerging doubts, concerns about their child's *"eternal security"* in cases of suicide, increased risk of suicide on the part of the Surviving Parent. Also, parents may immediately respond with a hopeful exclamation that their child was a Christian, but conceal their own doubts or evidence to the contrary. This may

234

foster increased fear and trepidation which they may be afraid to discuss. *...And, the NUMBER ONE thing to NEVER say to a Surviving Parent:*

Number 1: *"We can't always understand God's Will."*

• Response: This implies that God was either complicit in, or the perpetrator of, the child's death. Due to free will, millions of things happen on earth each and every day that are not God's will. Implying or asserting that everything that happens is *"God's Will"* can lead to anger at, and even hatred and rejection of God. It is obscenely presumptuous for a claim you know God's will for someone else.

Ten Things

There are Ten Things to NOT be said

To Moms and Dads whose kids are dead;

Ten Things that make it hard to cope;

Ten Things that rip away all hope.

Ten Things that people often say,

To try to take the pain away.

Sincere, but harmful to the heart;

So please take note so you can start

To be a help to Dads and Moms

Who don't know where peace will come from;

Who've suffered the worst kind of pain:

A loss that leaves a horrid stain.

"We Must Trust in God's Perfect Will."

Those painful words, they haunt me, still.

For not all things are willed by God.

To think so is so very odd.

When He bestowed *"Free Will"* on man,

It brought about a Perfect Plan.

But not all things are good and just:

Like greed, and hate, and damning lust.

But if man could not utter *"No."*

His *"Yes"* would have no meaning, so

Because man chooses to rebel
Our sin can lead us straight to hell.

It's not His Will that we should die,
Apart from Him; that is a lie.
Our loss is steeped in our foul sin.
That's true in the world we live in.

"Was He a Christian?" Often asked
By many burdened with the task
Of counseling sad parents who
Do what all hopeful parents do.

They hope and pray if they don't know.
Their fear and pain they oft don't show.
For they may have some dreaded doubt,
So better to leave this one out

Of your initial look in to
What healing task that you may do.
To raise some doubt about the fate
Of children whose folks now must wait

Is ill-advised: a risk at best.
'Tis better to find out first, lest
Your well-intentioned questions lead
To deeper fear, and painful need.

"God Gives, But Then He Takes Away"
Are words that lead to deep dismay.
Because it says to parents lost
That their child's life might be the cost

Of their own sin, or that God calls
On us to rob when darkness falls.
Or, that somehow the circumstance
Or person, or an act of chance

Was God's Design to take our joy;
To sweep away our girl or boy;
To leave us here with empty hearts;
To steal our peace, and tear apart

Our very lives; It's just not true.
Because God does not try to do
That which destroys us, He'll make whole
Our wounded heart; our shattered soul.

He did not take my Son away.
And there's no doubt that he will stay
Beside me, and due to His Grace
I'll one day see my Sweet Boy's face.

"Oh, No! Please Tell Me How He Died."
When I heard that, I sat and cried.

Because it seemed that he who asked
Was focused on the morbid task

Of finding out the lurid facts,
Not healing pain, or sharing acts
Of simple kindness, peace, and love,
Or bringing Comfort from above.

So, friend, I beg you, please don't ask;
Don't burden parents with the task
Of giving details at a time
When loss is new, it is a crime.

They'll give to you what is their need
To share, so that they can be freed
From having to relive the day
That tragedy took joy away.

"You Were the Perfect Mom and Dad."
These words can make a parent sad,
Because regret is always there;
A fear that somehow their best care

Was not enough to guard their child.
Regret is bred in guilt defiled.
No matter how a parent tries,
The doubt within them always lies.

It's better to bring focus to
The richness that they always knew
Was there between them in the days
They had together; God will raise

Them to some comfort later on,
But never will the pain be gone.
They won't get past it, but they can
Use it to be a better man

Or woman, and to use their pain
To help restore a peace again
To other parents who have lost
All hope due to a horrid cost.

"I'm Sure You Did All You Could Do."
Again, these words just don't ring true
To any parent who has gone
Through such a loss; It's just plain wrong

To make assumptions when they might
Have made mistakes or had a fight
With their child just before their death.
Don't say these words, they'll rob the breath

Of any hope for peace and rest
In troubled souls, because the best

Is not enough to thwart the thief.
These words can oft prevent relief.

"At Least You Have Another Child."
To say "that stinks!" is just too mild.
Because each child's a unique gift,
A parent's love can never shift

Away from one child to the next.
To say these words may truly wreck
The chance for you to help their soul.
Their loss has left a gaping hole.

"I Know Just How You Feel Right Now."
When I heard this, I "had a cow."
No other loss is like this one.
To lose a daughter or a Son

Is not intended, and obscene.
I know these words aren't meant as mean,
If you've not suffered this great loss,
Then you don't know just how it costs

A grieving parent all their hope,
They've lost all tools they need to cope.
They've lost all hope, and peace and joy,
It died there with their girl or boy.

"In Time You'll Overcome This Pain."
Believe me, this most horrid stain
Will always be there, and will lie
Inside their heart until they die.

Death of a child will always hurt.
So, please think first before you blurt
Out promises which can't be kept.
No child-based mem'ries may be swept

Away into forgotten rooms,
So, don't be one who then assumes
That time can heal and cast afar
A parent's pain who has those scars.

"At Least He's in a Better Place."
No matter, this is out of place.
While this might be their true belief,
These words don't always bring relief.

For we can't know if they're without
That nagging voice; that haunting doubt.
And also, while it may be true,
Their time with their sweet child is through.

And, sometimes this straddles the fence
Of facts which aren't in evidence.

Because the parent may feel dread,
Now that their precious child is dead.

So, now you know what NOT to say
When death takes parents' hope away.
It's not enough to teach you how
To NOT respond, so listen now:

What I can say, as one who knows,
The most horrendous of life's woes
Is that the sadness never ends.
But these kinds words from closest friends

Have helped to ease my deepest loss,
At night when I would turn and toss.
Such simple words felt from the heart
To me, whose life was torn apart

That dreaded day I got the word;
Forever changed the day I heard
My Son was killed, still in his prime;
Not from a crash, not from a crime;

But due to folks who came to try
To help, not strangers passing by;
But closest friends, and one who came;
Their lives will never be the same.

Here's what to say to those you love
When you are sent by God Above
To offer comfort and to care,
When they are trapped in deep despair:

"I cannot know how you must feel;
I only know my pain is real.
I feel so helpless, and would give
My life if your sweet child could live.

"To me you are so very dear;
If you'll allow, I will stay near
To hold your hand and cry with you.
I know these words are very true:

"My heart is broken, and I weep.
You're in my heart, and I will keep
You in my prayer; I mourn your grief.
I pray God brings, to you, relief.

"And if you're angry, that's okay
With God, beside you He will stay.
You're ever in my grieving heart.
I want so much to be a part

"Of healing, I won't leave your side.
In my heart you do now abide.

My heart is broken, my sweet friend.
My love for you will never end.

"To hearts where grief will always stay
I wish to take the pain away,
But I know this I cannot do.
Please know, my friend, that I love you."

My thanks go out to all of you
Whose open minds and hearts will do
All that you can to not destroy
All Hope of God's Returning Joy.

Chapter Thirty-Three

How to Pray for Surviving Parents

I do not profess to be a great theologian; merely a competent one. The lessons and insights I cite are based upon my perspective as a suffering, Surviving Parent who loves God, and who believes he has been called according to God's Purpose. And so, my theological friends and colleagues, if you disagree with the following opinions and interpretations, that's okay. I look forward to *"hunkerin' down"* to discuss and debate with you, at your earliest convenience. Know that I also strive to remain open and teachable. Thanks for listening, and considering what I offer. I realize it is likely to fly in the face of some reader's theological perspective.

Is it enough to simply do the best we can when we intercede for others? How should we pray for Surviving Parents? Excellent questions! First of all, going straight to the Word for answers, I find that if we do not know how to pray about something, we are to ask God for direction. Often times, that direction is somewhere in that Divinely-Inspired book. Romans 8:26 (ESV) tells us:

"Likewise, the Spirit helps us in our weakness. For we do not know what to pray for as we ought, but the Spirit Himself intercedes for us with groanings too deep for words." And, in James 1:5 (ESV), the Author tells us:

"If any of you lacks wisdom, let him ask God, who gives generously to all without reproach, and it will be given him."

The same goes for faith. If we lack faith, we need to use what little we have to ask for sufficient faith to see us through our adversities. In meditating on these Scriptures, my mind goes to Mark 9: 20-24, when Jesus encountered a desperate father whose Son was suffering from a lifelong spiritual problem, manifested by convulsions, seizures, and foaming at the mouth. The father asked Jesus to heal his Son. Jesus replied, *"If you can believe, all things are possible to him who believes."* The desperate father, in tears, cried out, *"Lord, I believe; help my unbelief!"*

And so, the moral of these stories is that God wants us to bring what faith, belief, and wisdom we have to the table, and if it is not enough to get the job done, or is faulty, He is faithful and just to give us what we need, if we ask Him. And so, I believe that the first step in knowing how to pray for Surviving Parents is to acknowledge and confess our lack of ability to fully empathize and handle the problem, and to ask God how He wants us to pray. Then do what He says. Therefore, I recommend in starting out your own prayer by confessing that you don't have a clue as to how to pray about the situation, and to ask God to take the wheel.

Secondly, we should acknowledge not just God's knowledge and understanding, but also his Empathy, Compassion, and Mercy; for, within His Mercy lies His capacity to ease pain and suffering. As I have said before, if anyone knows what a Surviving Parent is going through, it is God…***Because Someone Killed His Kid, Too.***

Remember the part where I talked about how many things that occur on this planet outside of *"God's Permissive and/or Ultimate Will?"* I believe that it is important to acknowledge to God that, whether or not what occurred was His Will, you rest on His Power and Control to use the Ugly Death that came out of

Man's *"Free Will,"* and to turn the tables on *"old Split Foot,"* who seeks to kill, destroy, corrupt, and usurp God's Will, His Kingdom, and those He loves the most: Us. Remember that God is NOT an equal Adversary to *"The Thief."* To believe that God is equal-and-opposite to Satan promotes a false belief of Duality: And, Satan LOVES it when people buy into that garbage.

So, let's get the Natural Division of Labor straight, shall we? God is THE Creator; the ONLY Creator. Lucifer was and is a creation that rebelled and was cast down out of Heaven when he got to be *"too big for his own britches."* To add insult to injury, Satan has never had an original idea, other than to rebel. He couldn't invent something if his life depended on it. In his factory and think tank, *"R & D"* does not mean, *"Research and Development,"* but rather, *"Rip Off and Duplicate."* He is a counterfeiter and a liar, who's has had a lot of practice.

So, in praying for Surviving Parents, give respective credit for the good and the bad according to *"who is responsible for what,"* and then lean on God's Majesty. You see, initially, before the fall of Lucifer and his rebellious minions, God taught Lucifer everything that Lucifer knew. However, he didn't teach Lucifer everything that GOD knew! At this point in my prayer for fellow Surviving Parents, I claim Romans 8:28 (ESV):

"And we know that for those who love God all things work together for good, for those who are called according to His Purpose."

Read that one carefully: Notice that the verse does NOT say that *"all things are good,"* or *"all things work for good."* The verse is not a promise for everyone. It is a specific promise for a special population of people: *"Those who are called according to His Purpose"* (Remember the story of *"Claudia's Spaghetti Sauce?"*) It is also important for us to pray for their marriage to not only survive, but to thrive…as well as for God to guard them from common problems that lead to the deterioration and destruction of most marriages, after the death of a child. A disturbing statistic: studies show that as high as 80% of marriages of Surviving Parents end within five years of their child's death.

In my research and experience, I have found three primary reasons for divorce among grieving spouses. First of all, *"silent resentments"* develop, often due to differences in personalities, and how respective parents choose to grieve over the loss of their child. For example, one parent may want to keep their child's room contents untouched, as a shrine or memorial to their dead child. The other parent, however, may want to honor their child by donating his or her possessions to another child in need, or to some other worthy cause. Therefore, each parent may argue that their spouse doesn't care enough about their devastating loss.

Secondly, parents sometimes blame each other, because of some action, or lack of action, that happened prior to the child's death, and which may have led to estrangement or conflict, or to their child's death. No matter whether or not the resentment is justified, it is difficult to effectively deal with those types of problems, when emotions are so raw, tender, and damaged.

Thirdly, and perhaps most significantly, parents sometimes isolate emotionally from their spouse, feeling that the death of their child is something that happened primarily to him or her, rather than to both of them, together. The very sight of their spouse constantly reminds them of their loss, leading to emotional avoidance of intimacy. A key danger sign is when either parent starts referring to their child as *"my child,"* rather than *"our child."*

Sometimes, these problems call for outside intervention; sometimes not. It is vitally important that those parents, as well as emotional caregivers who are trying to be supportive to Surviving Parents in their grief and bereavement, look for danger signs of relationship problems, and address them. These relationship problems will not likely go away by themselves. In the following chapter, I address why and how my marriage with Barb has survived, thrived, and flourished...and the lessons I have learned as I strive to daily fall in love and *"in like"* with my wife.

Remember that, at the point of acute, traumatic loss and suffering, such as in the loss of a child, many people aren't in the mood for a bunch of Scripture. Therefore, in light of the above observations, I recommend that you keep your prayers to yourself, unless it becomes abundantly clear that the Suffering Parents are wanting to hear the Word of God at that particular time. In your intercessory prayer, you are speaking to God on behalf of the grieving parents. Your prayer should be an honest and heartfelt communication, not a sermon. All too many times, we become guilty of preaching to others under the guise of talking to God.

Confess to God that you don't have the slightest clue what to do or say, and humbly ask him to guide you, according to *HIS* wisdom, not your own understanding. I have a sneaking suspicion that God will lead you to say to the person what I recommended in Chapter 31, at the conclusion of the *"Ten Things"* poem.

Chapter Thirty-Four

Falling "in Love, and in Like" with My Wife

The person who said *"We don't choose who we fall in love with"* is, in my humble opinion, only half-correct. I believe that while falling in love may sometimes be like walking around a corner and stumbling into a giant vat of warm honey, staying in love is usually a willful choice, that involves a lot of work and commitment. Over the last several years, after nearly eleven years of repeated, devastating losses in our lives, I've found myself doing something on a daily basis that may sound puzzling to you. I've been waking up each morning and asking God to assist me in falling *"in love and in like"* with my wife, all over again. Not only has it been a rejuvenating and exciting experience, it has been loads of fun! I fell in love with her for the first time on May 10, 1993... the day we met...which was, by the way, 53 days before I married her.

Over the last 26 years, I can't recall a day that I haven't been in love with her, although I can recall many regrettable moments when I didn't act like it...or when I did not deserve her devoted love for me. I'm coming to understand what it means to put substance and hard work into my emotional commitment and attachment to the very closest and precious of my loved ones: my blushing bride Barb. I'm bound and determined to get better at it.

Even more important, perhaps, than falling in love with her, I have found myself *"falling in like"* with her more and more each day. Barb is my closest confidant; my best friend. I would rather spend time with her than any other human being. I miss her when I'm not with her for even a day, and I can feel my face light

253

up with a smile, each and every time we are reunited. I have come to realize that, unlike most marriages that fall apart after the death of a child, ours is even stronger today than it was prior to Adam's death. Barb has remained by my side, as a faithful companion and *"help meet."* On top of that, I think she's hot. She still turns my head after 26 years. And, she cracks me up.

Since January 8, 2009, I've lost my Son, most of our household possessions (after our roof decided to move next door during a tropical storm), a former *"closest friend"* of 33 years (who betrayed Barb and me by defrauding us out of $12,000), my favorite pickup truck of all time, our dream travel trailer, my credit rating, and have nearly lost my right leg once, and my life twice, in vehicle crashes that for all intents and purposes should have killed me. I've overcome skin cancer several times. I believe in, and have faith in, far fewer people than I used to...but I believe in God even more, and my faith has never been stronger. Also, I have never, for even a moment, lost my assurance that Barb loves me and wants the best for me...in spite of myself.

I have gained and regained the loyalty, trust, and friendship of a handful of people who are more precious than gold to me. I've experienced miracle after miracle, blessing after blessing, and I am daily reminded of God's Comforting, Loving, and His Ever-Attentive Presence. Sometimes, though, due to the singularly-most horrible loss of my life, Adam's death, I yearn to *"blow this popsicle stand,"* when my grief is at its worst.

But, just when I think the pain is more than I can bear, I am reminded of the #1 item on tomorrow morning's *"To Do List:"* To wake up and fall in love and in like with my wife all over again, just like I did yesterday morning. It's a dirty job, but somebody's gotta do it, right? So, friends, family, and readers I've never met: please go and do likewise. Uh, let me clarify my instructions: don't fall in love with MY wife...fall in love with your own...or your husband. I have first and ONLY *"dibs"* on Barb, because she is...

My Best Friend and My Blushing Bride

(Written on Our 21st Anniversary – July 1, 2015)

I still recall how I did feel;
When her sweet smile my heart did steal.
And how my heart was whisked away
The morning of our wedding day.

For less than two months: fifty -three
Days to the day she *"glamoured me,"*
Before we stood and took our vows.
It's like it just did happen now.

It's twenty-one years, to the day,
Since we wed, and she's always stayed
Beside me better and for worse,
So I owe her a special verse.

My *"Blushing Bride"* she is to me;
Still now, I kneel on bended knee,
Because after these many years,
She *"turns my head"* and calms my fears.

She works so hard and makes me free;
Before herself she places me.
Deserving better than I am;
She tolerates my *"sense of ham."*

She makes me laugh; she makes me smile.
She always goes the extra mile.
She stops for turtles in the street;
I think that is so very neat.

She cooks, she sews, she gives her all;
She saves most critters, big and small.
There are exceptions to that path:
Roaches and gators earn her wrath.

Her love for *NASCAR* drives me nuts.
And most of all, I am a putz
Since love of pro-football began;
To that game she's a major fan.

She is so very proud to be:
The Loyal Wife of l'il ol' me.
I hope I can now give her all
That she deserves, 'cause I stand tall

And proud to say that in my life
I have her, she's my Loving Wife.

"We're legal now, it's twenty-one."
I think that we should have some fun!

But rather that goof off all day,
We'll no doubt work the hours away.
But then again, it's not a pain
To spend my day with her again.

No matter what the chore or job;
No matter how rude is the mob;
No matter how we're flanked by jerks;
Our sense of humor always works.

It's much to say that after all
These years, when troubled times do fall,
I know that she's there by my side:
My Best Friend and My Blushing Bride.

Copyright 2015, Joel Johnson

Chapter Thirty-Five
Some Thoughts on the Resurrection

Here's my take on something I read a long time ago about the truth of the Resurrection, in a book written by Josh McDowell: Josh pointed out that lots of people, down through the ages, have died for a lie...but... they believed that the lie was the truth. It's one thing to be willing to knowingly LIVE a lie, but quite another to be willing to lay down your life for a lie you KNOW is a lie. Take Islamic-extremist suicide bombers, for example. They're dying and murdering for a lie...but they believe it's the truth. If, for example, they could see that all of the *"70 virgins"* waiting for them were ugly, middle-aged, sweaty guys already burning in hell, they might not be so willing to explode a bomb in their own underpants. That's right, Loser! I called you the *"Underpants Bomber."* Put THAT in your shorts and smoke it!

Someone who claims that he or she saw something as an eyewitness, but knows that he or she did not see it....is a liar. So, here's the deal: ALL of Jesus' disciples were eye witnesses to the crucifixion of Jesus...and retreated, scattered and went into isolation...in despair. That was on a Friday. A little over a day and a half later, on Sunday morning, things changed when all but Judas (who committed suicide), in their own time, eye-witnessed the Resurrection of our Risen Lord Jesus. Each of the surviving disciples spent extensive amounts of time talking to Him after the Resurrection....and swore to it to all who would listen...for the rest of their lives! It was not a case of mistaken identity where they were fooled by a look-alike. They walked, talked, and were taught by Jesus for over a month after He walked out of that tomb. They were either ultimately-credible, truthful, reliable eyewitnesses to the Resurrection...or they were calculating, deceptive co-conspirators in history's most elaborate hoax!

Please, ponder this: After the crucifixion, they were hopeless, despondent, and defeated. Yet, a few days later, they were transformed into bold and effective evangelists and emissaries of the most beautiful and life-transforming message the world has ever experienced: Jesus is the Christ...the Son of the Living God...and He Lives! They all went on to become Apostles, joined by Paul (the Apostle Formerly Known as *"Saul"*), and all but one of them died a horrible martyr's death because they would not renounce the Truth of the Resurrection. Not one of them caved to pressure. None turned their backs on the Gospel. They devoted the rest of their natural lives to professing to all who would listen that Jesus is the Risen Son of God...and is their Lord and Savior. They never retracted... even while being imprisoned, mocked, reviled, tortured, and killed. The one who didn't die a martyr's death (John the Beloved) died in exile on Patmos.

Bottom line: IF the Resurrection was a hoax, the Apostles KNEW it was a hoax. Yet, they died indescribably horrible deaths, while proclaiming the Words of Truth that give Glorious Hope to us all: CHRIST HAS RISEN! They changed the world! If the Resurrection was a lie...logic dictates that at least one of them would have denied the Resurrection to save his own life. Today, I reside in Hope of the Resurrection. I can only make it through each day since MY Son was killed because of that Hope and Glorious Truth. If there is no Resurrection, there is no hope. I am so very thankful for the Truth. It has set me free.

260

Chapter Thirty-Six

Message to my Beloved Son
--written the day after Easter, 2014--

Dear Adam,

As I do every single day, I was thinking about you, loving you and missing you, and thinking about our Resurrection today, as I looked up to the sky. Here are a few post-Easter, *"way out of the box"* thoughts I wanted to share with you: For years and years, when thinking about *"dying to self,"* I have mistakenly focused on trying to suppress my temporal and selfish desires and wants, while ignoring that my desire to self-sabotage is at the core of my sinful nature. You, Son, who know me better than anyone, yet have always loved and excepted me unconditionally...know I have sometimes been unsuccessful, to say the least, in doing that.

My lack of success in that regard has largely stemmed from a misunderstanding of what it truly means to *"die to self."* Gradually, I am learning that it is much more than suppression of my selfish wants and desires. It involves a willful choice to repent of self-sabotage. It involves *"being transformed by the renewal of [my] mind."* My mind is made up of my will, intellect, and emotions. It is imperfect, to say the least. It is different from my spirit, which is, as a child of God, the Spirit of Christ. The negative forces around me have led to an *"understanding"* that I should be *"discouraged,"* which means to be separated and made unable to do the right thing. So, here's my decision: As for today, I choose not to lean on my own understanding. I choose to seek the Wisdom of God: a *"Peace that Passes All Understanding,"* a.k.a. an internal, God-inspired, and God-given Gift of internal Peace which just doesn't make sense, as far as the world is concerned. As for today, I choose to act, not merely react. I reject the external locus of control which has bound me. I choose to be challenged, inspired, encouraged, motivated, strengthened, launched, propelled, and driven by the very things which have disempowered, discouraged, and temporarily derailed me in the past. I choose to be resurrected.

That's my choice for today. And when tomorrow is *"today,"* may God grant me the wisdom, grace, and strength to make the same choice once again... because I have the sneaking suspicion the negative forces...those damned self-sabotaging internal voices, and the hassles, disappointments, and worldly problems, aren't likely to get suddenly and miraculously better. I hope they do, but I don't expect it. The thing is...it just doesn't matter anymore.

Since your death, ALL other losses have paled in comparison. They're mere annoyances. They're Gnats; Biting Flies; Skeeters. They are mere Zits, right before our Prom Date. Pains in the butt. My choice for today, inspired by you, is to accept the Gift of Encouragement given by our Heavenly Father. For now, until MY earthly death and resurrection, it is my *"way out of the box"* and my *"internal locus of control."* It's the *"Little Resurrection"* that I choose to recognize and greet each and every day, in order to overcome the supreme temptation to despise my life, and give in to *"Split Foot,"* better known as **"he who walks around in circles, and who seeks to devour me."** (Loose paraphrase of I Peter 5:8).

I thank our Father God for the Gift of that *"Daily*

262

Resurrection," that He grants when I first willfully submit to a *"Daily Death"* that I undergo when I am crucified with Christ. As Paul says in Galatians 2:20 (ESV):

"I have been crucified with Christ. It is no longer I who live, but Christ who lives in me. And the life I now live in the flesh I live by faith in the Son of God, who loved me and gave Himself for me."

I look forward to my Resurrection that I will one day experience, and THE Resurrection of His Son. Without Him, there is no hope, no meaning, no *"way out of the box."* As always...I love you, my son...I long to see you again, and, by the way, *"I still like the way you talk."* Happy Easter, Son!

Love, Dad

P.S. What in the world am I doing quoting Scripture to you? After all, you're sitting right there at the feet of the Guy who wrote it! Oh, and by the way, Son, here's another poem before I hit the road, written especially for you:

I Had the Chance to Be Your Dad

In midst of night I often long
To hear the beauty of your Song;
To know the joy and peace once more,
That came from standing at your door.

While listening as you would sleep,
I prayed the Lord your soul to keep
In His Hands, but I really meant
For you to live your life content.

I wanted you to always be
Right there, sitting upon my knee.
I wanted you to always live
Your life with all that I could give.

It's normal for a Daddy to
Wish all the best, and feel the true
Desire to shield, protect, and guard
His child from all that's cruel and hard.

To want to give his precious child
A pain-free world, so undefiled;
To make it his most precious chore
To ask God to forever more

Grant peace and joy and all the things
That living in His Pasture brings.
And so, I'd walk up to your bed
And place my hand upon your head.

In that soft touch, my soul had found
Beside your bed was Hallowed Ground,
Where I would place upon your chest
My hand to make sure you would rest

In safety, comfort, blessed peace.
I prayed your life would never cease
To know His Blessings and His Hand
Upon your life. I'd always stand

And tarry there just for a while.
Your face would cause my heart to smile.
I'd thank the Lord, as Daddies do.
Each night my soul you would renew.

I'd feel God's love and peace abound,
While you were safe in Sleepy Town.
I'd savor those most-precious times
When I'd begin with nursery rhymes,

And then would share God's Word, so dear,
While holding you, void of all fear.

For I could feel our deep, pure love:
A Precious Gift from God Above.

Years later, when you were a man,
Beside your bed I'd sometimes stand
To pray and soothe your troubled brow;
To whisper words I still hear now,

As though it happened yesterday.
Then…death took all my joy away.
Where once was light, 'twas now a hole
As darkness filled my ravaged soul.

No longer did I feel the joy
That came through you, my Precious Boy.
No longer did I hope or care,
As my heart filled with black despair.

But then, one night amidst the dread,
I felt upon my burrowed head
A gentle hand; I feel it now.
It often soothes MY troubled brow.

I feel your love and comfort born
Amidst the darkness when I mourn.
Our roles are now reversed, My Son.
You have become the Guarding One.

I feel your love, your joy, your peace;
I know your presence will not cease.
I know that on one future day,
He'll use your hand to brush away

The tears of sorrow ever more,
When I walk through His Heaven's Door,
And join you in His Blessed Place
Where we will both live in His Grace.

I'm often tempted to wish for
A chance to have you here once more.
But that's about MY pain and grief:
A Daddy's wish to find relief,

And, once again, having the time
To let you choose the nursery rhyme;
To wipe away the slightest frown,
As you drift off to Sleepy Town.

But, that would also mean that you
Would be back here, where you once knew
Such pain in your most-loving heart,
That anguish broke and ripped apart.

It, too, would mean you'd be the lad,
And I would be your loving Dad.

What we have now is more alive
Than human hearts can dare contrive.

Our bond will now forever last.
I'll one day soon forget the past,
And marvel at what lies ahead.
Forever we'll be free from dread.

A Universe of Peace above,
Forever in His Precious Love.
Until then, oft amidst my grief,
I feel your hand of sweet relief.

For now, your hand my brow has found,
As I drift off to Sleepy Town.
I'm now the child, you are the one
Who looks down on a troubled Son.

We've made full circle, you and I.
We'll someday meet up in the sky.
Until then, I remain so glad
I Had the Chance to Be Your Dad.

Chapter Thirty-Seven

My Final Thoughts…As I Sail Off into the Sunset

So, here I sit, all out of time;
But I will squeeze out one more rhyme.
My plan, my prayer, my wish, my hope
Is that this book will help you cope

With all your pain, and dread, and fears,
And loneliness, as darkness nears.
We've had some laughs, and also cried;
Please know that I've sincerely tried

To share my soul; my very heart.
I pray that I will be a part
Of all your lives, that you will see
How reaching out has made me free.

For it is true, that as we live
Our lives, it's much more blessed to give.
God's Gift to us, I do believe,
Is that, through giving, we receive.

It's time to go hide in my nook,
Because I've finished this here book.
And so, I hope my words take root;
'Cause writing this has been a hoot!

This final picture do I share,
As I recline in my soft chair.
I promise I won't brag or gloat,
Because, Dear Friends, It's Not My Boat.

In the famous last words of that great French Poet and Philosopher,
Porque Le Hogge…
Behdeh, Behdeh, Behdeh….That's All Folks!

APPENDICES

APPENDIX I

Adam's Eulogy

"On behalf of Deb, Barb, myself, and our families, thank you for coming here today to honor the memory of our Son, Adam. When I sat down to write this eulogy, I first prayed for strength and guidance, then wrote down some key words that applied to Adam:

- *Gifted;*
- *Talented;*
- *Brilliant;*
- *God-Sent;*
- *Unique;*
- *Belonging;*
- *Inspiring;*
- *Encouraging;*
- *Empathetic;*
- *Passionate;*
- *Loyal;*

- *Faithful;*
- *Helpful;*
- *Mischievous;*
- *Hilarious;*
- *Leroy;*
- *Tormented;*
- *Troubled;*
- *Hurting;*
- *And, of course…*
- *MUSIC !*

Our Son wanted desperately for his life to have significance. He wanted to make the world a better place; and he did. Sometimes he doubted that…but he couldn't have been more mistaken. There's ample evidence of that sitting in this room today. In one sense he hated his life because of his illness. But, in another sense he loved his life, largely because of many of you, and especially because of the love, sacrifice, and lifelong devotion of his Mom. She put Adam first his entire life, and he knew it. He loved us both very deeply. We never for a moment doubted that.

Like Paul, Adam asked God several times to remove his 'thorn in the flesh,' and was frustrated when it didn't go away. He tried to fix himself, but as hard as he tried, he felt like he was a prisoner of his own emotions and thoughts. Yet, in spite of his own personal pain, he continued to reach out to the disadvantaged, the hurting, and the vulnerable. He wanted to defend those who couldn't defend themselves. He saw injustice in the world, and wanted to make it right. He was passionate in his beliefs. I have so many stories to tell you about Adam. Some are hilarious, but I promised his Mom I'd tell only one: Adam accepted Jesus as his Lord and Savior on August 15, 1991, when he was only seven years old.

Several months later, I went to get him in Edmond, to take him on the road with me for a while, then to Florida, where I was residing. We were driving south on I-35 here in Oklahoma, just south of Purcell, when I looked over and saw that he looked very sad and troubled. I asked him what was wrong, and he said, "Dad, I saw the world's worst t-shirt." I asked him what he was talking about, and he told me that, earlier that day, he had seen a man wearing a t-shirt that said, "Jesus knows diddly." Adam was on the verge of tears as he asked me why someone would wear a shirt that said something as bad as that.

My heart was broken. I ached for him, as I silently prayed that God would give me the right words to say to mend my little boy's heart. I pulled over to the side of the road, put my arms around him and told him about Saul of Tarsus, and how, even while he was a great enemy of Christianity, Christians prayed for him. I told him about how Jesus appeared to him, and as a result,

Saul became the Apostle Paul, a great champion of the Faith. I told Adam that it was not God's will that any man should perish, and that, if we earnestly prayed for the man like the early Apostles prayed for Saul, that God would give that man with the t-shirt the opportunity to accept Jesus.

That seemed to satisfy Adam, and he made a promise to pray for the man with the t-shirt. I must confess that while that was my response to my Son, deep inside I wanted to go find that man who had grieved my Son's tender little soul and yank him through the key hole of his car door. As it turned out, Adam's heart for God was bigger than mine. We then prayed together for the man, then we headed down the road.

I remember that Adam, even as a small boy, always prayed silently, not wanting to recite his prayers out loud for his Mom and me to hear...so we never knew exactly who or what he was praying for. About six months later, Adam was with me again, and we were visiting an addiction treatment center in the Oklahoma City area. When we were sitting in a waiting room there, Adam said he had a question for me. He asked, "When will I know that it's OK for to stop praying for the man with the t-shirt?" You see, for six solid months, Adam had prayed every night for a man that he didn't even know. That was what Adam was all about. He prayed for each of you. That was something very special about Adam. He never gave upon praying for those of you whom he felt needed it most. He doubted his own worthiness, but even while he was the most doubtful, he cared for each of you; each in different ways.

Yes, Adam loved God. Some of you may not know that

recently Adam had decided that he wanted to complete college and go to law school...so he could champion the abused, and neglected people of the world, and to do something special for God. He thought if he could do that, he could really make a difference. As hard and as steadfast as we were in telling him otherwise, like so many of us, Adam didn't he know how truly significant his life was, and is, and will be in years to come. Sometimes he was angry at God and doubted Him. But he never lost God, and never stopped loving Him. He learned that, even though he was angry at God, God was not angry at him. And so we celebrate Adam's life, and although we mourn our loss, and hurt so deeply because we were and are a part of Adam...we know that he will always live inside us.

More than anything else, other than God and his family and friends, Adam loved music. He wrote many beautiful songs. The most beautiful of all, however, he actually co-wrote with God without knowing it. He wrote it a bit differently than he wrote his other music. He wrote it without his guitar, pen, or paper. He wrote it with his life. He never sang it. He never played it. He lived it. It's called, "The Notes of Adam's Song."

< <Recited Lyrics to Song, found on pp. 25-26>>

Each and every one of you here today is a Note in His Song, and you are also a Seed. You are here because of how Adam touched your lives. Adam's impact on your lives is also a seed. My prayer is that he did not die in vain. <u>So, in loving memory of Adam...go, and grow, in his honor.</u>"

Jesus replied: "The hour has come for the Son of Man to be glorified. I tell you the truth, unless a kernel of wheat falls to the ground and dies, it remains only a single seed. But if it dies it produces many seeds. The man who loves his life will lose it, while the man who hates his life will keep it for eternal life. Whoever serves me must follow me, and where I am, my servant also will be. My Father will honor the one who serves me."
...John 12:23 –(NIV).

APPENDIX II

Paying Tribute to Your Loved One

Over the last eleven years, I have spoken to many Surviving Parents who had engaged in some sort of memorial activity, in order to honor their departed child. Some of their efforts have been simple, one-time-only types of activities, while others have been more elaborate and ongoing.

In my own personal experience, I have found that writing this book, and seeing it published, has been an extremely important part of my healing process, as has been the publication of my poetry in various social media, publications, et cetera. I have come to understand that the activity is most meaningful when it ties directly into what was important to the Deceased, and/or when it does something positive to tie into the cause or manner of death. Here are some examples, including memorial projects actually enacted by Surviving Parents with whom I have been in contact, as well as those which are brainstorming ideas I have thought of. The *"world is your oyster,"* so to speak…limited only by your imagination…and by your personal resources, talents, and skills. Here are some ideas to consider:

- Establish, or join, a non-profit organization and/or charity to help others who have suffered catastrophic, or whose lives have been scarred by untimely loss of life of your Deceased Child. E.g. The National Crisis Intervention Training Institute, Inc.

- Support or provide training and education for law enforcement, clinicians, and/or other helping professionals, connected to an issue that was instrument-tal in your Deceased Child's death.

- Same as the above, focusing on prevention of issues relevant to the loss of your Deceased Child's life. E.g. suicide, addiction, chronic depression, et cetera. *Thank you, Kerri Mims!*

- Engage in the establishment of a memorial project to further the cause of something your Deceased Child found to be important. E.g. establishment of a shelter for feral animals, or a wild life preserve project. *Thank you, Jim and Alicia Maisano!*

- Establish or support some sort of educational project. E.g. a library, public awareness training program, financial scholarship, et cetera.

- Fund and/or erect some sort of functional monument in honor of your Deceased Child. E.g. a water fountain, park bench, et cetera, marked with an *"In Memory of..."* plaque.

- Fund and/or plant trees, gardens, et cetera, in honor of a Deceased Child who felt strongly about environmental issues.

- Helping others by participating in various *"mutual aid support groups,"* such as our own Surviving Parents Network, 12-Step problems for survivors of various forms of problems, et cetera.

One way of brainstorming, in order to come up with meaningful and therapeutic ideas is to communicate with friends of your Deceased Child, to further explore issues that your important to your child that you may or may not have been aware of. Another way is to utilize the Psychological Autopsy Family Worksheet, found in Appendix VII. Obviously, this tool is also there for your use, should you decide to request assistance from NCITI in performing a Psychological Autopsy or Therapeutic Psychological Autopsy, pertaining to your child's death.

SPECIAL NOTE:

Please feel free to communicate with me directly at *JJohnson@NCITI.org,* to offer ideas for other types of therapeutic memorial projects, and actual projects you have engaged in. If you wish to provide me with your name and photographs of your project, I will be happy to include your story in future Editions of this book, as well as in the *"Surviving Parents' Training Manual and Resource Guide,"* currently scheduled for publication in late 2020, or 2021.

Also, watch for updates on our website about our *Living Tributes Workshop*, either in your geographic area, or online, through our *Surviving Parents Network.*

APPENDIX III

Online Resources for Surviving Parents

Surviving Parents Network is a part of the *Notes of Adam's Song* program, within the *National Crisis Intervention Training Institute.* For more information, go to the *www.NCITI.org* website. Please contact the Author directly (at *JJohnson@NCITI.org*) to become involved in this group. Among other services, this program provides live, weekly online mutual-aid support meetings for Surviving Parents.

DISCLAIMER: The author has not had direct contact with all of the resources listed below, and therefore wants to stress that their being listed here does not constitute an endorsement by me personally, nor by NCITI, Inc. At the time of this book's publication, all of these websites were verified as being active.

...WEBSITES LISTED ALPHABETICALLY...

- *www.alivealone.org*

Provides educational resources for surviving parents and their families.

- *www.babysteps.org*

Provides a public online forum for Surviving Parents to post a memorium of their deceased child.

- *www.bereavedparentsusa.org*

This group has been around for about 25 years. It offers support to Surviving Parents and other family members, in the form of an array of services, with local chapters in many states. They also hold an annual national conference for bereaved families.

- *www.caringbridge.org*

Provides guidance to Surviving Parents who wish to start their own personal memorial website.

- *www.compassionatefriends.org*

  Offers local mutual-aid support meetings for Surviving Parents, in various locations throughout the U.S.

- *www.bearsofhope.org.au*

  Based in Australia, this website offers assistance to Surviving Parents who lost a child in childbirth.

- *www.grievingdads.com*

  Provides opportunities for Surviving Dads to post their remarks re: their deceased child.

- *www.grievingparents.net*

  This program is sponsored and run by the Grieving Parents Support Network, and is founded by Nathalie Himmelrich, the author of *Grieving Parents: Surviving Loss as a Couple.* Nathalie is a professional Grief Therapist, and also a Surviving Parent. Nathalie also is involved with the ***MWAH (May We All Heal) Online Support Group****.* You may seek out rmore information on that group via Nathalie's website.

- *www.mend.org*

  A Christian website, especially for *"Mommies Enduring Neonatal Death."*

- *www.mymiscarriagematters.com*

  Provides support to Parental Survivors of a misscarriage.

- *www.nationalshare.org*

  Provides information and resources for parents who have lost a child during early pregnancy.

- *www.nicuhelpinghands.org*

  Provides contact information for several organizations

who serve grieving and bereaving Surviving Parents.

- *www.opentohope.com*

  Provides an online forum for Surviving Parents.

- *www.pomc.com*

  The National Organization of Parents of Missing Children, Inc. provides an array of services focused on education, support, prevention, advocacy, and awareness, pertaining to special challenges faced by Surviving Parents who suffered loss of a child due to homicide.

- *www.sids-network.org*

  Provides support and resources for parents who have lost a child to Sudden Infant Death Syndrome (SIDS), and Other Infant Death (OID).

- *www.skylersgift.org*

  Provides financial assistance to Surviving Parents, for mortuary and funeral costs

- *www.stillstandingmag.com*

  An online magazine for bereaved parents and those suffering from infertility.

- *www.suicidepreventionlifeline.org*

  This website, associated with the Suicide Prevention Helpline (*1-800-273-8255*), provides a national network of 24-hour suicide prevention and crisis intervention services, for callers of all ages.

- *www.taps.org*

  Provides specialized services to Parental Survivors who currently serve in the military.

APPENDIX IV

A Preview of Coming Attractions

At the time of the publication of *"The Notes of Adam's Song: A Surviving Parent's Journey Through the Valley of the Shadow of Death,"* the Author is working on another book, with the working title of *"Called to Encouragement"* Stay tuned for that one, as well as the *"Surviving Parent's Operator's Manual and Resource Guide,"* a follow-up to this book, tentatively scheduled for publication in 2021.

I am including this essay in this book, because, over the years, I have learned that sometimes, encouragement is *"a matter of life or death."*

Called to Encouragement
(Chapter One: How to Drive Your Wife Nuts, in One Easy Lesson)

Sometimes I drive my wife, Barb, totally insane. Over the years she has learned to accept the things that she cannot change, and has found the courage, strength, and tenacity to change the things she can...but, sometimes, she still tenaciously clings to the false belief that she can change how I behave in public. Wrong!

Example: Whenever we eat out, she often refers to me -- facetiously, mind you-- as the *"Patron Saint of Restaurant Servers.* This stems from my long-held belief that a great Server is not just hard to find; he or she is a Treasure. A great one with a sense of humor and pleasant nature, is even harder to find. Serving food to people, especially in a very hectic environment, is a difficult job, with a steep learning curve. It is also one of the hardest jobs on the planet, and certainly one which is drastically under-rated, and under-appreciated.

It is also viewed by many who engage it as a way of making a living, as the best option they have, yet not one that they would select as their Chosen Profession. I have encountered many servers who feel trapped in their job, and who are undergoing tremendous pressures outside of work, such as providing a home for their families, balancing other responsibilities such as educational or vocational goals. It is so very easy for them to become discouraged, down-trodden, and emotionally defeated. The likelihood of this occurring, in my opinion, is exponentially equated to the level of rudeness and callousness they daily endure, inflicted by many of the jerks they have to *"wait on."*

I have come to realize that it is a major shot in the arm for all discouraged individuals to be, not only complimented for their performance, but to be educated as to why and how what they do for a living is so important. I believe in tipping well, but also in telling people why I tip them well. Understandably, that drives Barb a little crazy, too, but she never overrides my decision, and is fully supportive and tolerant.

Take it from a person who has spent many of days, months, and years eating alone in restaurants while *"on the road,"* how powerfully invigorating it can be to receive excellent service from a server who also takes a little bit of time to provide brief companionship, without sacrificing efficiency, and who is attentive to my needs. I do not merely provide *"labels"* to them, like *"you're a great waitress,"* but, rather, describe specifically what they did that was excellent, how it made me feel, and the positive impact it had on me...making it easier to do my job that day. That message is referred to as an *"I-Message."*

When I accurately describe their behavior, instead of labeling them, is harder for them to argue with the compliment. While I might be tempted to suffice with a label such as *"you're just super!"* they may be feeling like 120 pounds of sacked garbage: useless, valueless, and ready to be thrown away. Not only does my attempted compliment fall on deaf ears, it also causes them to have immediate doubts about my judgment. Their internal response is therefore likely to be, *"Mister, if you knew me the way I know me, you wouldn't believe that about me, and wouldn't want to have anything to do with me."*

Case in point: a recent conversation I had with an excellent server. She had asked me why I was in town; I told her I was providing training to law enforcement on investigative methods related to crimes against children. Rather than sitting there and basking in the compliments that she began to lavish upon me, I turned the tables on her, and re-focused on her, thanking her for helping me to do my job. She looked me and asked, *"How did I do that?"* I told her that, after over three decades of combatting the types of problems I face on my job, it is often difficult to get back up there and to be *"upbeat"* when I am speaking publicly. Dealing with such unsavory and depressing topics, it is important to appear enthusiastic, and to even break the down mood humor.

I told her that I had been watching her closely during my meal, and noticed that she was an excellent multi-tasker, engaged her customers well, was attentive, and didn't waste time, energy, or steps. I pointed out that I marveled at the fact that she did not once walk across the room toward a customer without stopping on

285

the way back to check on her customers' needs, to fill their coffee cup, and to bring a ray of sunshine into the room.

Then, I told her that I am usually tempted to just drive through a fast food place, because eating out by myself is often a drudgery, rather than a pleasure. I told her that because of her emotional support to me that morning, I felt energized, and that her performance will no doubt contribute to my ability to help children vicariously through the training I provide to law enforcement. I closed by saying that no person does their job by themselves, and that her role in my upcoming training was just as important as mine. I thanked her for being a part of my team that day, and rewarded her with a 50% tip.

Now, here's why I did that: First of all, what I was saying was the truth. Secondly, I had learned from a brief comment that she was raising three children by herself. I marveled at her resilience. Who knows how close she had been recently to throwing in the towel, giving up, and even running away from her family? Who knows how many nights she had lied awake, worrying about where the next meal or pair of shoes was coming from for her three children? Who knows how close she may have been to being suicidal? Had she been tempted to end it all, but was only kept alive of how her death would affect her children? Believe me: It was clear that he was a courageous woman.

Courage is not the lack of fear. It is having the ability and commitment to do the right thing, even when afraid to do so. As I have spent a lot of time meditating on what *"Courage"* truly is and is not, I have also thought about what the words *"Discouragement"* and *"Encouragement"* truly mean. Operating on my above-mentioned definition of *"Courage,"* let's look at the prefixes of those other two words. *"Dis"* means to separate from, or take away from; *"En"* means to add to or put into. Therefore, when we *"discourage"* someone, we don't just make them feel bad; we rob them of their ability and commitment to do the right thing, when they are afraid or too weary to do the right thing. On the other hand, when we "encourage" them, we aid in fulfilling and reinforcing their ability and commitment to do the right things, when facing the scary obstacle they face on a daily basis.

The importance of encouragement was one of the core skills that Jim Bogan and I addressed when training Support Counselors for the National Youth Crisis Hotline. We believe that it saved lives. You see, every good person, no matter who they are, desires to have significance in their lives. They want to matter, and to make a positive difference in someone else's life. I have come to believe that I have a special calling in my life:

I am *"Called to Encouragement."* In fact, I believe that every Christian has the same calling. Every day, I make a conscious effort to seek out at least three people I believe may need to be encouraged. I may never see the results; that is for God to know. Sometimes, I'm blessed to be told how I have made a difference. I have been shown on countless occasions, that Adam's efforts to restore dignity and hope to the lives of so many homeless people, and discouraged friends who needed it the most, were evidence that he, too, felt *"Called to Encouragement."* It is one of the many reasons that *"Adam's Song"* has so many beautiful *"Notes."*

APPENDIX V

Psychological Autopsy Protocol

Referral
- Request inquiry received / Intake Screening Short Form sent – received by Case Assignment / Intake Specialist

Intake
- Received form screened for eligibility & appropriateness by CA/IS -CFFI / Background Data Form sent / received

Triage
- Case triaged and assigned / Travel itinerary planned and coordinated with onsite liaiSon and/or RP

Field
- CFFI dispatched / primary & conducts collateral interviews / artifacts reviewed and analyzed / local officials consulted

Debrief
- CFFI debriefs family and introduces to (CM/ACS) / Notifies and coordinates w/ community referral resources

MDT Submit
- CFFI prepares final report rough draft and sends to IDT members for sign-off / Report sent to relevant agencies

MDT Staffing
- IDT Staffing / preliminary summary, of findings, collateral issue ID / Tx and aftercare recommendations

Final Submit
- Summary Final Report prepared and dispatched to selected MDT members / Staffing date / time announced

APPENDIX VI

Therapeutic Psychological Autopsy Protocol

Refer
- Request inquiry received / Intake Screening Short Form sent – received by Case Assignment / Intake Specialist

Intake
- Received form screened for eligibility & appropriateness by CA/IS -CFFI / Background Data Form sent / received

Triage
- Case triaged and assigned / Travel itinerary planned and coordinated with onsite liaiSon and/or RP

Field
- CFFI dispatched / primary & conducts collateral interviews / artifacts reviewed and analyzed/ local officials consulted

Debrief
- CFFI debriefs family and introduces to (CM/ACS) / Notifies and coordinates w/ community referral resources

MDT Submit
- CFFI prepares final report rough draft and sends to MDT members for sign-off / Report sent to relevant agencies

MDT Staffing
- MDT Staffing / preliminary summary, of findings, collateral issue ID / Tx and aftercare recommendations

Final Submit
- Summary Final Report prepared and dispatched to selected MDT members / Staffing date / time announced

Follow-up #1
- Case management and aftercare services initiated / data gathered, analyzed, and anomized for reporting

Follow-up #2
- 90-day aftercare follow-up evaluation to determine plan adherence and efficacy / treatment plan modified p.r.n.

Follow-up #3
- 180-day and 360 day follow-up evaluations to determine plan adherence and efficacy / modification / added referrals

Case Closed
- 2-year follow-up with family / if appropriate, family members invited to become Peer Support Mentors

Copyright 2014, Joel Johnson

289

APPENDIX VII
To Families Requesting a Psychological Autopsy

INTRODUCTION
(Please Read Carefully)

Dear Parent(s), Guardian(s), and/or Grieving Family Member(s):

You, or a designated family member, have requested the services of our Psychological Autopsy Team. **Our job is to better help you understand your deceased loved one's state of mind in the weeks, days, and hours leading up to his/her death, and to, if at all possible, help you find answers to haunting questions that you may be having.** Unlike most psychological autopsy protocols, our approach is multi-disciplinary in nature, allowing different specialized professional perspectives to examine the data, and to contribute to a more holistic, complete, honest, and revealing picture.

Our decision to initiate an active Psychological Autopsy begins with our team gathering and evaluating information provided by you. At your request, we will send you a .pdf document entitles the *"Psychological Autopsy Family Worksheet,"* for you to print out, reproduce, and distribute to adult members of your family, as well as *"significant others."*

Information requested in the *NCITI Psychological Autopsy Family Worksheet* Includes:

- Reporter/Historian Information
- Brief Narrative Overview of Circumstances of Death
- Decedent's Past and Present Demographic Information
- Photograph(s) of the Decedent
- List of Relevant Parties and Contact Information
- Investigative Agencies and Reports
- Relevant Artifact Evidence (Held or Released by Agencies)
- Available Official Reports
- Available Artifacts Retained by Family Members
- Decedent's Family History and Structure

- Credit and Financial History (Decedent's and Family's)
- Decedent's Life Routines
- Decedent's Hobbies, Interests, and Extracurricular Activities
- Decedent's Social History
- Decedent's Employment History
- Recent and Historical Changes in Decedent's Life
- Parental Impressions of Decedent's "Thought Life"
- Decedent's Known Physical / Mental Health History
- Known Medical or Other Clinical Concerns
- Psychological / Psychiatric / Behavioral Problems
- Decedent's Spiritual History and Beliefs
- Problematic Mental Health Treatment History
- Stressors in Decedent's Life
- Decedent's Past and Current Legal Difficulties
- Decedent's Substance Abuse / Dependence History
- Decedent's Known or Suspected Sexual History
- Decedent's Known or Suspected Sexual Abuse History
- History of Decedent's Self-Injurious and/or Threatening Thoughts, Ideations History
- Family's Suicide, Homicide, and other Significant Death Histories
- Additional Details/Circumstances of Decedent's Death
- Circumstances that Led to Request for Psychological Autopsy

Upon receiving and reviewing the completed forms, our Chief Forensic Investigator will review the material, and notify you whether or not we are able to conduct the investigation. If we are not able to honor your request, we will notify you of the specific reasons that the investigation is either being delayed, or declined. The outcome and actual process of our investigative approach is designed to provide the following:

- Answers to the haunting, damning questions which often plague surviving family members.
- A holistic picture of your deceased loved one's psychological, emotional, cognitive, physical, familial, social, and spiritual conditions which may have led up to his/her death.

- A gathering, organization, and processing of relevant information and resulting findings, and determination as to how they may apply to the other clinical or legal investigations into the circumstances of your deceased loved one's death, by law enforcement, the medical examiner's office, the district or state attorney's office, etc.
- The benefit of having the details and circumstances--as well as the reports from the above-mentioned agencies--examined and scrutinized by professionals from several different fields of expertise.
- Tools and information which will hopefully assist you in grieving, mourning, and healing.
- An assessment of possible or probable problems and obstacles to healing which you may be facing in upcoming weeks, months, and years, with recommendations regarding support services and other available resources at your disposal.
- An assurance that your concerns are not being ignored, and that you are not alone.

It is also designed to be therapeutic and healing in nature, while not interfering with, or compromising the integrity and effectiveness of any official investigation of the circumstances of your loved one's death. Any or all of the following types of information will be gathered during the investigation, and will be interpreted, evaluated, synthesized, and applied to your child's case by our multi-disciplinary team:

- Identifying demographic information, both past and present.
- All available investigative reports by law enforcement, forensic laboratories, and any civilian investigative businesses and/or organizations.
- Information regarding the significant events leading up to, and contemporaneous to your deceased loved one's death, including those considered directly applicable to his/her frame of mind, as well as collateral social and familial events which may have had primary or secondary impact upon his/her life, or the lives of significant others.

- Detailed information regarding your deceased loved one's family history, marriages and other significant relationships, past and present illnesses, injury history, medical history, mental health history, credit and financial histories, and evidence of prior history of self-injurious thoughts, ideations, gestures, and/or attempts.
- Detailed information about any other family members, close friends, or significant others who have attempted suicide, or have died as a result of suicide or homicide.
- Evidence of your deceased loved one's "thought life:" his or her fantasies, dreams, thoughts, delusions, fears, hopes, plans, et cetera.
- Recorded artifacts such as journals, blogs, financial records, correspondences, diaries, web pages, entries via social network websites such as Facebook, Instagram, et cetera.
- Information regarding your deceased loved one's known sexual history.
- Evidence of any recent or historical changes in eating habits, weight gain or loss, hobbies, employment, or other extracurricular activities, and other life routines.
- Any noted changes in your deceased loved one's circle of friends and social contacts, as well as information regarding sustained friends, associates, romantic or sexual partners, confidants, et cetera.
- Information about your deceased loved one's known methods of coping with stress, escape-based avoidance methods such as substance abuse, running away, et cetera.
- Recent stressors, and difficulties (e.g. legal, social, financial, romantic, et cetera).
- Any circumstantial or other collateral evidence which may help to determine intention on the part of your deceased loved one.
- Examination of death-inducing methodology, including a lethality risk assessment, examination of nomenclature of the mode and instrument(s) of death, et cetera.
- Assessment of family members' and significant

others' reaction to the decedent's death, at the point of notification, and afterward.

- Statements and evidentiary reports of other assigned investigative and clinical professionals.
- Interviews with clinicians and other helping professionals who attended to your deceased loved one prior to death (such as counselors, therapists, social workers, teachers, tutors, mentors, etc.

Obviously, the gathered information may be sensitive, private, surprising, or even shocking to you. **It is very common for family members to feel the need to be protective of the memory of their deceased loved one, and/or to protect the reputation and privacy of the family.** For that reason, they may sometimes be tempted to withhold or alter information or evidence. **First of all, we want to assure you that THE UTMOST DISCRETION AND CARE is taken to protect the INTEGRITY, PRIVACY, AND CONFIDENTIALITY of you, your family members, and the memory of your deceased loved one.**

We also want to assure you that we will be exceptionally careful to make sure that **you will receive all the support and help that you need to process the discovered information, as well as the final outcome findings of our investigation.** False, misleading, partial, or withheld information may result in erroneous findings, as well as improper recommendations. For those reasons, **we implore you to be as open, honest, candid, and complete as possible in providing the requested information.** To us, there is no such thing as too much information, as long as it is potentially or actually relevant to our investigative inquiry.

This information will assist us in making some preliminary determinations, to appropriately assign relevant personnel to your case, as well as to streamline the process as much as possible, and to formulate key interview questions. **It is by no means complete. It is only a collection of beginning reference information for us. More will be learned from the actual interviews that we conduct with you, other family members, friends, involved professionals, witnesses, et cetera.**

While the questionnaire is only the beginning of our investigative inquiry, you will no doubt find its completion to be a time and effort-consuming process, which may sometimes be emotionally, psychologically, cognitively, and spiritually difficult. **We ask you to take your time in completing the following questionnaire / worksheet. Once you have completed it, set it down in a private, secure place, then go back to it in a day or so, re-read what you have written, and see if there is anything you would like to add or amend.**

Please feel free to contact us at any point of the documentation process, if you require assistance in completing any or all sections, and/or in clarifying your responses. On behalf of our team, thank you for your cooperation in providing this information, which we are confident will prove to be an invaluable tool in accomplishing our task of helping you.

With deepest condolences, empathy, respect, and appreciation,

Joel Johnson

Joel Johnson, M.A.Ed.
Director / Chief Field Forensic Investigator
NCITI Psychological Autopsy Team
--Also, a Surviving Parent Since January 8, 2009--